CAT CORA'S | kitchen

CAT CORA'S kitchen

Favorite Meals for Family and Friends

Cat Cora with Ann Krueger Spivack

photographs by Maren Caruso

CHRONICLE BOOKS

SAN FRANCISCO

Library of Congress Cataloging-in-Publication
Data available.

ISBN 0-8118-3998-2

Manufactured in Singapore.

Designed by Public
Studio prop stylists: Maren Caruso, Kim Konecny, and Erin Quon
Location prop stylist: Hilary Brodey
Food stylists: Erin Quon, Kim Konecny
Photo assistant: Faiza Ali

Distributed in Canada by Raincoast Books
9050 Shaughnessy Street
Vancouver, British Columbia V6P 6E5

10 9 8 7 6 5 4 3 2 1

Chronicle Books LLC
Second Street
San Francisco, California 94105

www.chroniclebooks.com

This book is for my family, especially my grandmother Alma, both kindred spirit and steadfast friend. I miss you every day.

TABLE OF CONTENTS

10   Introduction

12   THE CORA KITCHEN IN JACKSON, MISSISSIPPI

15   Getting my mom to cook *kota kapama* for my brother's birthday • *I've bribed him to ask for my favorite meal*

16   **Chicken Stewed in Wine, Garlic, and Cinnamon** (KOTA KAPAMA)

18   **Butter and Cheese Noodles** (MAKARONIA)

19   **Caramelized Brussels Sprouts**

21   **Tomato, Cucumber, and Feta Salad** (HORIATIKI)

22   **Olive Oil Cake** (LATHI TORTE)

25   Sharing my family's two secret ingredients for pork • *Bourbon and my grandmother's mustard give this roast its zing*

26   **Spring Onion, Fennel, and Potato Soup** (PATATOSOUPA)

27   **Slow-Roasted Pork with Bourbon** (HIRINO PSITO)

28   **Southern-Style Greens** (HORTA)

30   **Walnut Tart** (KARITHI TARTA)

33   Roasting a chicken with lemon and herbs • *The Zouboukos brothers cook an old-fashioned church supper, Jackson style*

34   **Fish Roe Spread with Crostini** (TARAMOSALATA)

35   **Classic Greek Roasted Chicken with Lemon and Herbs** (KOTOPOULO PSITO)

36   **Church-Style Lemon-Roasted Potatoes** (PATATES LEMONATES)

37   **Stewed Green Beans with Fresh Oregano** (FASSOULAKIA YAHNI)

38   **Milk Pie** (GALATOBOUREKO)

41   Slow-smoking a beef brisket • *Greek flavors take on a Southern flair when my dad cooks*

42   **Pork Skewers with Pita Bread** (SOUVLAKI ME PITA)

43   **Spiro's Brisket** (VODINO SPIROS)

45   **Greek Potato Salad** (PATATOSALATA)

46   **Bell Peppers Stuffed with Meat and Rice** (PIPERIES YEMISTES ME KIMA KAI RIZI)

48   **Greek Butter Cookies** (KOURAMBIEDES)

53 Arriving in Skopelos • *Aunt Demetra is worried we'll be hungry*

55 **Spinach, Dill, and Feta Baked in Phyllo Dough** (SPANAKOPITA)

57 **Artichoke Hearts Braised in Lemon Juice** (ANGINARES ME LATHOLEMONO)

58 **Cucumber Yogurt** (TZATZIKI)

59 **Spicy Feta Spread** (HTIPITI)

61 **Sour Cherry Torte** (TORTES ME VISSINO GLYKO)

65 Cooking a classic *stifatho* with my Aunt Demetra • *This Greek stew calls for rabbit, wine, and beautiful pearl onions*

67 **Stewed Rabbit with Pearl Onions** (KOUNELI STIFATHO)

70 **Polenta with Fontina and Parmesan**

71 **Fresh Spinach with Preserved Lemons** (SPANAKI ME LEMONE)

72 **Honey-Dipped Cookies with Fresh Figs** (MELOMAKARONA KAI SIKA)

75 Stopping at a taverna after wandering through town • *Sampling shrimp with capers, Aegean meatballs, and baklava orthi*

77 **Shrimp and Caper Salad** (GARITHOSALATA ME KAPPARI)

78 **Aegean Meatballs with Pita Bread** (KEFTETHAKIA KAI PITA)

79 **Cabbage Leaves Filled with Lamb and Rice** (DOLMATHES ME ARNI KAI RIZI)

80 **Skopeletti Stuffed Tomatoes** (DOMATES YEMISTES)

81 **Rolled Baklava** (BAKLAVA ORTHI)

85 Roasting a whole fish • *I cook for one of my inspirations, Jacques Pépin*

87 **Whole Fish Roasted with Fennel, Olives, and Chilies** (PSARI PSITO)

90 **Tomato Bread Soup** (DOMATO SOUPA ME PSOMI)

92 **Pampered White Beans** (FASSOLIA)

94 **Grilled Asparagus with Tangerine Aioli** (SPARANGI TIS SKARAS ME MANTARINI SALTSA)

96 **Orange-Scented Almond Cookies** (AMYGTHALOTA ME PORTAKALI)

99 Making a harvest chicken with fresh grapes and *vinocotto* • *This meal reminds me of the Gypsies in Greece and the grape crush in California's wine country*

101 **Spicy Gypsy Mussels** (MYTHIAS)

102 **Rustic Kalamata Olive Bread** (ELIOPITA)

104 **Grilled Grape Leaves Filled with Goat Cheese** (DOLMATHESTIS SKARA ME TIRI)

106 **Harvest Chicken with** *Vinocotto* (KOTO ME VINOCOTTO)

107 **Strawberry-Topped Vanilla Custards** (CREMOSAS)

111 Pan-searing a halibut to go with a sweet corn zabaglione • *The flavors of summer—sweet corn and tomatoes—shine in this meal*

112 **Summer's First Heirloom Tomatoes with Fresh Mozzarella**

113 **Pan-Seared Halibut with Sweet Corn Zabaglione**

116 **Banana-Coconut Cream Pie**

119 Serving *achibades* with *vitello* (clams and fennel-cured salami with breaded veal) • *My own version of surf and turf, with an affogato for dessert*

121 **Manila Clams with Fennel-Cured Salami** (ACHIBADES)

122 **Breaded Veal with Tomatoes, Garlic, and Basil Brown Butter** (VITELLO SCALLOPINI)

123 **Fava Bean–Mint Ravioli with Fava Bean–Mint Pesto**

125 **Baked Stuffed Onions** (KREMITHES YEMISTA)

127 **Warm Chocolate Ganache over Coffee Ice Cream** (AFFOGATO)

131 Fishing for compliments at my seafood fest • *Cooking just about every type of seafood and pulling out all the stops*

133 **Crab and Avocado "Sandwiches" with Mango Coulis**

134 **Prawns in Grappa Cream Sauce with Salsa Rosa**

136 **Split Lobster Stuffed with Crabmeat** (ASTAKOS SPIROS)

137 **Spicy Broccoli Rabe**

139 **Fresh Fruit Tart**

143 Combining a velvety duck breast with exotic black rice • *Adding pistachios and oranges to black rice makes this my favorite restaurant meal*

145 **Salt-Roasted Beet, Arugula, and Endive Salad** (PANTZARIA SALATA)

146 **Muscovy Duck Breasts with Black Rice, Pistachios, and Orange**

148 **Prunes and Armagnac with Vanilla Gelato** (VANILA PAGATO ME THAMASKINO KE ARMAGNAC)

150 MY KITCHEN AT HOME

153 Packing up a wine country/tailgate party picnic • *Cooking both hearty and delicate foods for alfresco meals*

155 Tomato Croquettes with Cucumber Yogurt (DOMATOKEFTETHES ME TZATZIKI)

156 Lamb-and-Cheese-Stuffed Sandwiches (ARNI KAI MYZITHRA SKOPELOS)

158 Watermelon, Feta, and Mint Salad

161 Sipping spirits with Greek mezes • *Set out mezes, or small plates, and bring out the ouzo*

162 Taki's Cured Sardines with Tomatoes, Olives, and Bread (SARDELES TAKIS)

165 Skillet Leek Pizza (TIGANOPITA ME PRASO)

167 Baked Eggplant with Meat and Béchamel Sauce (MOUSSAKA)

169 Custard-Filled Phyllo Triangles (BOUGATSA)

171 Firing up my famous all-grill supper • *Friends help carry my dining table into the backyard*

173 Grilled Artichokes with Caper Aioli (AGGINARES SKARAS KAPPORI SALTSA)

174 Grilled Prawns with Egg and Lemon Froth (GARIDES TIS SKARAS AVGOLEMONO)

176 Grilled Lamb Chops with Alma's Fruited Mustard (ARNI TIS SKARAS ME MOUSTARTHA)

178 Skopelos-Style Grilled Potatoes (PATATES ME LEMONE)

181 Grilled Stonefruit with Prosciutto and Sheep's Cheese (VEIKOKO SKIN SKARAS ME TIRI)

182 THE PANTRY

184 Roasted Chicken Stock

185 Roasted Veal Stock

186 Pickled Mushrooms (MANITARIA TURSI)

187 Alma's Sweet-Hot Mustard

188 Preserved Lemons

189 Basil Oil

190 RESOURCES

192 Acknowledgments

196 Index

204 Table of Equivalents

INTRODUCTION

Every chef has a kitchen that shaped his or her ideas about food and life. For me, one kitchen set me on the path to becoming a chef, and another kitchen changed my views on how I cook. The first was my parents' kitchen in Jackson, Mississippi, and the second was the kitchen of my aunt Demetra and uncle Yiorgios on Skopelos, one of the Aegean Islands in Greece.

When we began writing this book, it focused on cooking on Skopelos, and how working in a kitchen in Greece changed how I cook. But we kept returning to the Jackson, Mississippi, kitchen, and I realized that my cooking reflected what I'd learned in both kitchens. Not just cooking skills but how I felt about life and family, what the best moments in life were about for me.

In Jackson, my mother and father were part of an extended family of Greeks for whom cooking and eating were the center of life. If you've seen the movie *My Big Fat Greek Wedding,* you have a sense of the warmth and humor in a community of Greek Americans. You also get the idea that every social occasion centers around food. Not just any food. Greek food.

Greek cuisine is seeing a renaissance in the United States right now. You might think you know *spanakopita* or baklava, but unless you live in a Greek community, chances are the *spanakopita* and baklava you've tasted are pale imitations of what they can be. Thirty years ago, people in this country thought of Italian food as pizza and tinny-tasting red sauce on overcooked spaghetti and meatballs. Now, we all know the names of different pasta shapes and we understand the variety in good Italian cooking. Americans are on the verge of discovering the flavors of true Greek country cooking. Taste a golden brown *spanakopita* made with mounds of fresh spinach and dill, and you'll see the foods of Greece in a new light.

The first part of this book shares traditional Greek foods cooked in an American kitchen—an American kitchen in the South, which gives the preparations an additional spin. (My relatives in Greece don't add mustard and bourbon to their pork roast as we do on page 27, but this very Southern combo is what makes the roast so tender and flavorful.) I've put my favorite foods into the menus in this section, both to give you a sense of what life is like in a kid-filled Greek American kitchen and to help you decide what to serve when you make these dishes.

The recipes in the first section are the easiest recipes in the book, but there's still skill involved in making Milk Pie, page 38 (a custard surrounded with layers of phyllo, baked, and finished with a piping hot lemon syrup—like a phyllo-wrapped crème brûlée). We've given clear, detailed instructions in this section on everything from working with phyllo dough to smoking a beef brisket.

The second section of the book takes you to Greece, where we feature recipes for dishes prepared as they have been on Skopelos for centuries. Visiting Skopelos in 2000 and filming my relatives for the Food Network television show *My Country, My Kitchen* was a turning point for me as a chef. On previous visits, I'd eaten Skopelos foods with abandon but not with any serious thought about cooking these foods myself. This time, tasting with years of experience as a chef, I realized that we Americans were missing some of the key flavors. I decided to bring these stories and these foods back with me to both my restaurant kitchens and my kitchen at home.

The recipes in the third section include the most popular meals I've made in my Northern California restaurants: clams with salami (page 121) and veal in a basil brown butter (page 122), duck breast and black rice (page 146), velvety *cremosas* topped with strawberries (page 107). These recipes are a bit more challenging, but each one has been geared for the home cook. The dishes in this section have the depth and complexity of a great restaurant meal, but can be made without the conveniences of a restaurant kitchen.

Finally, the last section of the book includes some of my favorite foods for entertaining at home. I've included my unusual warm stuffed sandwich, made by hollowing a large loaf of bread, filling it with diced lamb sirloin and cheese, and cooking the meat right inside the bread (page 156). This sandwich makes me the hit of every Super Bowl party. On the same menu, you'll find delicate tomato croquettes (page 155), which I made for my first James Beard dinner. You'll also find my all-grill menu on page 171: gorgeous lamb chops, lemony potatoes, stone fruit wrapped in prosciutto and cheese—all recipes designed to be cooked over a grill while you sit outdoors chatting with your friends and drinking fine wine.

For me, that sums up the idea of home entertaining—an evening is more fun when the menu includes something unusual and unexpected, but the cook shouldn't ever miss out on her or his own party.

Cooking is a funny thing—it's both personal and universal. The recipes in this book take you on a journey that begins in Jackson, Mississippi, and ends (for the time being) in Northern California. My quest to be a chef began in Jackson, where I was lucky enough to meet Julia Child and Marion Cunningham. Both women took the time to patiently answer all my questions about cooking, working in restaurants, being a chef. For years I would look back on that encounter with amazement that two people who didn't know me would spend so much time talking to a young woman who hadn't yet begun training to be a chef.

Years later I had the chance to meet Jacques Pépin while cooking in the Napa Valley. Showing the same generosity of spirit I'd found in Julia and Marion, he said something that has stayed with me ever since. Jacques said, "The people who take the time to become very good cooks deep down want to take care of other people." I think of my mother and father and also my grandmother, Alma, all of whom were very good cooks without any formal training, and I begin to understand why these recipes have come to mean so much to me.

I hope they come to mean something special to you as well.

—CAT CORA

The Cora Kitchen in
JACKSON, MISSISSIPPI

Both of my families—my family in Jackson, Mississippi, and my family on the island of Skopelos in Greece—share a love of good food, a passion for gathering around a table for long conversations with family and friends, and a generosity of spirit that reaches from the Aegean Sea to the American South. My dad, Spiro, born in the Mississippi Delta two months after his parents left Skopelos, has the warmth and fun-loving appetite of a Greek and the humor and charm of a Southern gentleman. With my dad at the head of the table, even the simplest meal is a guaranteed good time.

My mother, Virginia, comes from a long line of good home cooks. When she married my dad, she set out to re-create the dishes that he ate as a kid. She made savory dishes like *kota kapama*, chicken cooked slowly in a savory sauce of tomatoes and onions with a hint of cinnamon (page 16). She baked *galatoboureko*, a custard wrapped in flaky pastry and topped with bubbling hot lemon syrup (page 38). In Greece, *galatoboureko* is a classic dessert, every bit as beloved as baklava, and yet in the United States few people have heard of it. These Greek dishes served up with Southern flair were the flavors of my childhood, and until I became a chef I didn't realize how much I'd learned from my mom.

Both my parents worked—my father taught high school history and my mother was a nurse—yet even with limited amounts of time and money, they fed us great meals and made a nightly family dinner a priority.

My other influence in the Jackson kitchen was Alma Brothers, my mother's mother. I was in junior high when my mom went to graduate school for her doctorate. Alma came to stay with us to help out while my mother buckled down, handling her job and her studies. My mom earned her degree, but we couldn't bear to let Alma leave. At that point she was my biggest ally, always there to help me hold my own, and many of my favorite recipes began with her.

The dinners of my childhood inspired me to write this book, to pass along the idea that good cooking can spring from modest budgets. Greek home cooking—whether on Skopelos or in Jackson—has always meant wonderful fresh flavors from inexpensive ingredients.

I came back to these foods after training to be a chef and found, to my surprise, that *kota kapama, galatoboureko,* and all the recipes in this section of the book stand on their own merits. These dishes aren't just sentimental favorites or dishes made to stretch tight budgets, but great food that brings new flavors and new meaning to home cooking.

MENU

16 • Chicken Stewed in Wine, Garlic,
and Cinnamon (KOTA KAPAMA)

18 • Butter and Cheese Noodles
(MAKARONIA)

19 • Caramelized Brussels Sprouts

21 • Tomato, Cucumber, and Feta Salad
(HORIATIKI)

22 • Olive Oil Cake (LATHI TORTE)

GETTING MY MOM TO COOK *KOTA KAPAMA* FOR MY BROTHER'S BIRTHDAY • I've bribed him to ask for my favorite meal

My mom always worked, and yet somehow, every birthday, she pulled out all the stops and made exactly what we wanted for dinner. What I wanted, every year, was *kota kapama*. Exceptionally tender and flavorful, *kota kapama* is one of those dishes that sits on the back of the stove all afternoon, filling the house with lush aromas. I liked it so much, I'd bribe my younger brother, Chris, to ask for it on his birthday, too. This is a dish that I loved as a kid and still love today.

Together, the garlic, onions, and cinnamon create a rich flavor that's intensely savory, but still homey and comforting. I like to serve *kapama* with wonderfully buttery noodles and cheese, but it's also good over rice, orzo, or any kind of pasta (my dad is passionate about *kota kapama* with long macaroni).

You probably don't request Brussels sprouts for your birthday dinner, but, for me, well-caramelized Brussels sprouts with fresh lemon juice and capers are a treat. This recipe gives them just the right texture and great flavor. Even people who turn down Brussels sprouts without a second thought won't let this bowl pass by.

My salad of choice for this menu is *horiatiki*. Cucumbers, tomatoes, onions, feta cheese, and Kalamata olives in a lively vinaigrette—these ingredients are what come to mind when you think of Greek salad. My family loves to dip bread in this vinaigrette, so the recipe makes plenty.

The Greeks have made breads and cakes with olive oil for thousands of years, so my family's recipe for a spectacularly moist olive oil cake pays tribute to those early Greek bakers. The best thing about this cake is it stays moist and buttery for days—although in my house it seems to vanish within hours.

I think this melding of cinnamon, onions, and garlic is addictive. As *kota kapama* simmers on top of your stove, it fills your home with an aroma so heavenly, when you sit down to dinner you wonder if it can taste as good as it smells (yes, it can). This dish is definitely one of my favorite ways to cook chicken.

If there's one thing you can do to make your *kapama* taste like mine, it's skip the supermarket shrink-wrapped chicken. Either buy a whole bird and cut it yourself or seek out your local butcher and have him or her cut your chicken for you. Fresh-cut poultry always makes the biggest difference in how *kapama* tastes.

For a true *kota kapama,* finish the dish with the aromatic sheep's cheese, Myzithra (see Resources on page 190). If you can't find Myzithra, use kasseri cheese or freshly grated Romano.

Chicken Stewed in Wine, Garlic, and Cinnamon • KOTA KAPAMA

I chicken (2 ¹/₂–3 pounds), cut into 8 serving pieces

I teaspoon ground cinnamon

2 teaspoons kosher salt

I teaspoon freshly ground black pepper

5 cloves garlic

2 tablespoons extra-virgin olive oil

4 cups coarsely chopped yellow onions

¹/₂ cup dry white wine

2 cups water

One 6-ounce can tomato paste

¹/₂ cup grated Myzithra cheese

Pat the chicken pieces dry with paper towels so they don't spatter in the pan. Mix the cinnamon, salt, and pepper together in a small bowl and rub the chicken pieces on all sides with the mixture. Mince 3 of the garlic cloves and set aside.

Heat the olive oil in a large, deep, nonaluminum skillet over high heat. A 12-inch skillet with sides about 3 inches high will allow you to brown all the chicken pieces at once. If you don't have a skillet large enough, brown the chicken in 2 batches, using I tablespoon of oil for each batch. Don't crowd the pieces in the pan or the chicken will steam rather than brown.

Add the chicken to the skillet and brown for 4 to 5 minutes on each side, shifting the pieces with a metal spatula so the chicken doesn't stick to the skillet. When the pieces are nicely browned on all sides, remove from the pan and set aside.

Reduce the heat to medium-high and add the onions and minced garlic. Cook for about 3 minutes, stirring constantly, until the onions have softened and are a rich golden brown. Add the wine and scrape the bottom of the pan with a spatula or spoon to deglaze, loosening any browned bits.

When the wine has evaporated, add the water, tomato paste, and remaining 2 whole garlic cloves. Return the chicken to the pan. The liquid should cover about three-quarters of the chicken. Reduce the heat to low, cover skillet with a lid, and simmer for about I hour, or until the chicken is tender and thoroughly cooked. (If the sauce becomes too thick, thin it with a little more water.) Taste and adjust the seasoning.

I like to serve this with my family's homemade buttered noodles (see page 18) but it's also great over rice, orzo, or macaroni. Sprinkle the grated cheese over the top of each serving.

SERVES 4

Why serve plain pasta when a little cheese and butter give noodles so much more flavor? I rarely serve *kota kapama* without these rich, savory noodles. Because at my house pasta, butter, and pecorino are always on hand, I sometimes make a simple dinner from these noodles and a big green salad. See Resources on page 190 for specialty cheeses if you don't have a full cheese market near you.

Butter and Cheese Noodles • MAKARONIA

I tablespoon kosher salt, plus I ¹/₂ teaspoons

10 ounces egg noodles, elbow macaroni, penne, or rigatoni

3 tablespoons unsalted butter

3 tablespoons grated sheep's cheese (kasseri or pecorino), plus ¹/₂ cup for serving

¹/₄ teaspoon freshly ground black pepper

In a large saucepan, bring 4 quarts of water to a boil. Add I tablespoon of the salt and the pasta and cook until al dente, 5 to 7 minutes. Drain.

In a large sauté pan, melt the butter over medium-high heat. Add the drained pasta and the 3 tablespoons grated cheese. Season with the remaining salt and the pepper and toss well.

Top with the remaining cheese and serve hot.

SERVES **4** TO **6**

Brussels sprouts are definitely underrated. I'm always amazed when people pass them up without even tasting them. I love the challenge of making Brussels sprouts irresistible. My secret is to really let them caramelize in the brown butter. Don't just give them a stir or two. Keep them in the pan until the outer leaves are crispy and the insides are tender and delicious.

Caramelized Brussels Sprouts

Stem the Brussels sprouts and peel off any wilted or bruised outer leaves. With a paring knife, cut a shallow X into the stem end to help the sprouts become a bit more tender during cooking. Cut each sprout in half.

3 pounds Brussels sprouts

1 tablespoon kosher salt, plus 1 teaspoon

4 tablespoons unsalted butter

1/4 cup capers, drained

2 tablespoons fresh lemon juice

1/2 teaspoon freshly ground black pepper

2 tablespoons grated Parmesan cheese for garnish

In a saucepan, bring 2 quarts of water to a boil, then add 1 tablespoon of the salt and the Brussels sprouts. Cook until tender when pierced with a knife, about 10 minutes.

In a large sauté pan, melt the butter over medium-high heat and cook until golden brown. Add the sprouts. Cook for about 10 minutes, constantly moving the sprouts from side to side until they're well caramelized on all sides.

Remove from the heat and add the capers, lemon juice, pepper, and the 1 teaspoon salt. Sprinkle with the cheese and serve.

SERVES **4** TO **6**

The classic Greek salad of cucumbers, tomatoes, and red onion slices, this version of *horiatiki* is my favorite because the vinaigrette, or *lathoxitho*, is so good. This recipe makes plenty of *lathoxitho* because my family likes to dip bread into it when the vegetables are gone. My favorite non-Greek, Jennifer Johnson Cora, taught me to top this salad with sautéed garlic, caramelized until sweet and crisp.

Tomato, Cucumber, and Feta Salad • HORIATIKI

4 large cloves garlic, minced

1 tablespoon extra-virgin olive oil, plus 1 cup

3 large ripe tomatoes, cored and cut into $1/4$-inch slices

1 large cucumber, peeled and cut into $1/8$-inch slices

1 small red onion, cut into thin slices

12 Kalamata olives

1 cup crumbled feta cheese

$1/2$ cup red wine vinegar

1 tablespoon chopped fresh oregano

Kosher salt and freshly ground black pepper to taste

In a small sauté pan, sauté the garlic in the 1 tablespoon olive oil over medium-high heat, stirring often, until the garlic is caramelized and slightly crunchy. Set aside and let cool to room temperature.

Arrange the sliced vegetables on individual plates or a platter. Top with the olives and the crumbled feta.

Whisk together the vinegar, 1 cup olive oil, and oregano. Season each salad with salt and pepper, drizzle with the dressing, and top with the sautéed garlic.

SERVES 4 TO 6

Greeks first baked bread when the very first sailors brought Egyptian flour home. Until the Middle Ages, all Greek breads were made with olive oil, so our *lathi torte* recipe has centuries of tradition behind it.

Like a pound cake, this smooth, citrus-flavored torte is so incredibly moist that it doesn't need anything extra—no icing, no glaze—it's perfect all by itself. If you like, dust confectioners' sugar on top, and if you really want to dress it up, top with fresh berries and whipped cream. The olive oil in the recipe gives you the richness of butter with much less fat, and the cake stays moist for days.

Olive Oil Cake • LATHI TORTE

2 tablespoons unsalted butter, melted

$1/2$ cup all-purpose flour

$1/2$ teaspoon baking powder

$1/2$ teaspoon baking soda

I teaspoon kosher salt

3 large eggs

2 cups granulated sugar

$1 1/2$ cups extra-virgin olive oil

$1 1/4$ cups whole milk

$1/4$ cup Grand Marnier or other orange liqueur

$1/4$ cup fresh orange juice

I tablespoon grated lemon zest (see note)

$1/2$ cup finely chopped blanched almonds

Confectioners' sugar for dusting (optional)

Place the rack in the middle of the oven and preheat to 350°F.

Brush a 10-inch round nonstick cake pan with the melted butter. If your pan isn't nonstick, butter the bottom of the pan, line it with a round of parchment paper, and butter the parchment. Set aside.

Sift together the flour, baking powder, baking soda, and salt. Set aside.

Place the eggs in the bowl of a stand mixer fitted with the whisk attachment. Whisk the eggs for several seconds at medium-high speed. Add the granulated sugar and whisk for I minute more. Reduce the speed to medium and pour in the olive oil, then the milk, Grand Marnier, orange juice, and lemon zest.

When all the liquid ingredients are incorporated, add the dry ingredients. Mix until the batter is smooth, stopping as necessary to scrape down the sides and bottom of the bowl. Fold in the almonds. Pour into the prepared pan.

Bake for I hour, or until a wooden skewer inserted in the center of the cake comes out clean. Remove from the oven and let cool on a wire rack for 5 minutes.

Run a knife around the sides of the pan and invert the cake onto the back of a baking pan. Remove and discard the parchment paper. Turn the cake right side up onto a serving platter. When the cake has reached room temperature, garnish with a dusting of confectioners' sugar, if desired. Cut into wedges and serve.

Note: Much of the flavor of an orange (or a lemon, lime, or grapefruit) comes from the colored portion of the peel. Be sure to scrub the fruit before zesting. If you don't have one, invest in a zester, which makes quick work of shaving fine bits of the peel, and leaves behind the peel's bitter white underside.

SERVES I2

MENU

26 • Spring Onion, Fennel, and Potato Soup
(PATATOSOUPA)

27 • Slow-Roasted Pork with Bourbon
(HIRINO PSITO)

28 • Southern-Style Greens (HORTA)

30 • Walnut Tart (KARITHI TARTA)

SHARING MY FAMILY'S TWO SECRET INGREDIENTS
FOR PORK • Bourbon and my grandmother's mustard give this roast its zing

I call this my close-to-home and around-the-world menu because each dish figures big in the South, and yet you can find variations in every corner of the world.

Take roasted pork, for starters. I've tasted terrific pork in Greece, Mexico, Italy, and France, but for my money, Southerners have the edge. This gloriously tender, slow-cooked pork can thank bourbon for its deep, savory flavor. My grandmother's mustard gives it a pop, with just the right mix of heat and spices.

Potato soup is another homey food that can change drastically with just a few added ingredients. Spring onions and fennel make this version just right as a starter to the succulent pork.

Greens, too, conjure up images of the South, but this recipe comes to Jackson via Skopelos. At an early age, the *Skopeletti* learn to gather wild greens from the hillsides around their homes, and I think my love of fresh, fresh greens has come right across the ocean to me. The freshness of your greens—and a sharp eye so they don't overcook—matters more than what kind of greens you use. This very simple recipe enhances the flavor of every variety of greens.

I finish this meal with a walnut tart, my uptown rendition of that old Southern favorite, pecan pie. I like the flavor of walnuts, especially now that I can find really fresh nuts grown near my home in Northern California (see Resources on page 190). Combining the crunch of walnuts with a delicious brown sugar filling, this dessert ends the meal on a winning note.

I like the thought that these homey Southern staples can be homey in other parts of the world, too.

The clear spiciness of fresh fennel and delicate green spring onions provide just the right complement to young potatoes. Yukon gold potatoes work perfectly for this soup, but you can use a wide variety of potatoes and get great results.

With the onions, too, you have a bit of leeway. I like to use spring onions when they're available, but don't feel you have to file this recipe away for most of the year. Just substitute boiler onions if spring onions aren't in season, and you'll have a heartier soup that's great on chilly days.

This recipe serves six to eight people easily, but even if you're cooking for only two or four people, you'll be glad for the extra—it tastes even better reheated for lunch or a light supper the next day.

Spring Onion, Fennel, and Potato Soup
◆ PATATOSOUPA

I medium fennel bulb with fronds (about $3/4$ pound)

$1/4$ cup plus I tablespoon extra-virgin olive oil

3 cups diced spring onions or boiler onions

I tablespoon minced garlic, about I large clove

2 tablespoons finely chopped fresh thyme

$1/4$ cup white wine

2 cups heavy cream

2 cups whole milk

12 small or 4 large boiler potatoes such as Yukon gold (about I $3/4$ pounds), peeled and quartered

3 cups water

I tablespoon plus I $1/2$ teaspoons kosher salt

$1/2$ teaspoon freshly ground black pepper

Trim the ribs and bottom stem of the fennel bulb, removing any brown or bruised parts. Reserve the fronds (the lacy green tops of the fennel) for the garnish. Chop the bulb into medium dice.

Combine the olive oil, onions, and fennel in a large saucepan over medium-high heat. Sauté for 8 to 10 minutes. Add the garlic and thyme and cook for just about 30 seconds to bring out their flavor. Pour in the wine, cream, and milk and bring to a boil. Stir in the potatoes and return to a boil. Reduce the heat and simmer, covered, until the potatoes are tender when pierced with a knife, about 20 minutes.

Puree the soup in a blender. (This should probably be done in batches, depending on the size of your blender. Err on the side of caution, pour small batches into the blender, and be sure to hold down the lid because hot soup can cause the lid to pop off.) Return the pureed soup to the pan, add the water, season with the salt and pepper, and bring to a simmer to heat through and blend the flavors.

Pour the soup into bowls and arrange a small fennel frond or two on top just before serving.

SERVES 6 TO 8

Juicy inside with a wonderful crust outside, this pork is so incredibly tender, it tends to fall apart during slicing—not a problem if you serve it with steaming hot mashed potatoes, polenta, or even cheese grits.

To be sure the meat absorbs all that great garlic and sage flavor, season your pork and add the garlic and sage leaves the night before you roast it. I season most roasted meats the way I do this one, cutting small slits and stuffing them with garlic and herbs to flavor the meat while it cooks. I prefer pork butt or shoulder when slow-roasting; don't use a lean cut like a pork loin because it will dry out during cooking.

Slow-Roasted Pork with Bourbon•
HIRINO PSITO

2 tablespoons kosher salt

I tablespoon freshly ground black pepper

I pork butt or pork shoulder (5 pounds)

10 cloves garlic

10 fresh sage leaves

I cup all-purpose flour

2 tablespoons extra-virgin olive oil

$1/2$ cup Alma's Sweet-Hot Mustard (page 187)

$1/2$ cup firmly packed brown sugar

4 or 5 dashes Worcestershire sauce

$1/4$ cup bourbon whiskey

Mix the salt and pepper together in a small bowl and rub the pork on all sides with the mixture. Make 5 slits on the bottom of the roast (the lean side) and stuff each one with a garlic clove and a sage leaf. Turn the roast over and repeat on the top, or fatty, side. Wrap the roast in plastic wrap and refrigerate overnight.

Preheat the oven to 250°F.

Pour the flour onto a plate, unwrap the pork, and roll it in the flour, coating all sides of the meat. Pat off any excess flour. Heat the olive oil in a large, heavy skillet over medium-high heat. Cook the meat on each side, including the ends, until golden brown. This will take about 15 minutes.

Transfer the meat to a roasting pan. In a bowl, combine the mustard, brown sugar, Worcestershire sauce, and bourbon. Stir until smooth.

Coat the meat with one-half to two-thirds of the mixture, using enough to cover all sides of the meat. Reserve any remaining sauce. Cover meat with aluminum foil and roast for about 4 hours. Remove the foil and spoon the remaining mustard-bourbon sauce over the top of the roast. Return to the oven, uncovered, and roast an additional 2 hours, or until the meat is completely tender and falling from the bone.

SERVES **6** TO **8**

Greens taste different wherever you go. The best *horta* I've had I gathered with Greek relatives, all of us carrying baskets and stooped over, scouring the hillsides of Skopelos. Even from island to island in Greece, the flavors of greens can vary widely, and they're certainly distinct in every region of the United States. The simple cooking method in this recipe works no matter what kind of greens you're cooking, from turnip to collard to dandelion. I like extra-citrusy greens, so I squeeze on extra juice just before serving. You can substitute vinegar for the lemon—especially a Southern-style chile-infused vinegar—if that suits your mood.

In Greece, the greens rarely need to be trimmed because only young tender plants are gathered for cooking. When picking your own greens, go for the youngest, most tender leaves. If your greens have large ribs, cut them away using a paring knife.

Southern-Style Greens • HORTA

2 pounds wild greens such as escarole, chicory, mustard, rocket, dandelion, or a mixture of greens, tough stems or large ribs removed

$1/4$ cup extra-virgin olive oil

$1/4$ cup plus 2 tablespoons fresh lemon juice

Freshly cracked black pepper to taste

Bring a large saucepan three-fourths full of salted water to a boil. While the water heats, wash the greens carefully to remove sand and dirt.

When the water boils, add the greens and cover. Cook just until the greens are tender, 4 to 5 minutes. Take care not to overcook them. Place a colander in the sink and drain the greens immediately. Let cool for 10 minutes.

To serve, drizzle the greens with the olive oil and lemon juice and finish with cracked black pepper.

SERVES **4** TO **6**

Dough

I large egg, beaten

I teaspoon vanilla extract

2 ¹/₂ cups all-purpose flour, plus extra
for dusting pan

I ¹/₂ cups granulated sugar

¹/₄ teaspoon salt

10 tablespoons well-chilled unsalted
butter, cut into small pieces

Filling

3 tablespoons all-purpose flour

¹/₃ cup firmly packed brown sugar

¹/₈ teaspoon freshly grated nutmeg

¹/₈ teaspoon ground cinnamon

5 tablespoons unsalted butter

¹/₃ cup dark corn syrup

I egg, lightly beaten

I teaspoon vanilla extract

¹/₂ cup walnuts, toasted (see note)
and roughly chopped

Toasting Nuts: You can toast nuts in a skillet on top of the stove but I like to spread nuts on a baking sheet and toast in a 375°F oven. The heavier the nut the longer it stays in the oven. Pine nuts burn quite easily so don't take your eyes off of them—they usually toast in just a minute or two whereas walnuts can take five to seven minutes. Use your eyes and your nose to determine when the nuts are perfectly toasted. As soon as you catch a whiff of their fragrance and you see the nuts begin to color, stay alert because they can become overly toasted very quickly.

In Jackson, pecan pie was a Southern favorite. Now that I live in California, I make this refined version with crunchy, locally grown walnuts. Fantastically fresh walnuts make all the difference with this recipe. If you don't find great walnuts at your local grocer, see Resources on page 190.

This is one of those desserts that can follow a casual meal or a more formal dinner. To dress it up, just top with vanilla gelato and a drizzle of caramel or a spoonful of fresh whipped cream.

You can make the dough with either a food processor or an electric mixer; we've described the steps for each method below.

Walnut Tart • KARITHI TARTA

To make the dough in a food processor: In a small bowl, beat together the egg and vanilla and set aside. Combine the flour, granulated sugar, and salt in the processor and pulse for 3 seconds to blend. Put the chilled butter pieces in the processor and pulse with the dry ingredients until the mixture is the consistency of a coarse meal. Turn the processor on and pour the egg mixture in a steady stream into the feed tube. Run the processor just until the dough forms a compact ball. Immediately turn the processor off and turn the dough out on a flat surface. Form into a disk about I inch thick and wrap with plastic wrap. Allow the dough to chill and rest for at least I hour in the refrigerator.

To make the dough in an electric mixer: In a small bowl, beat together the egg and vanilla and set aside. Place the flour, sugar, and salt in the bowl of a stand mixer fitted with the paddle attachment. Blend the dry ingredients on low speed for I minute. Add the chilled butter pieces and mix until the mixture resembles cornmeal or coarse crumbs. With the mixer on low speed, pour the egg mixture in a steady stream into the flour mixture. Mix just until the dough forms a compact ball. Immediately turn the mixer off and turn the dough out on a flat surface. Form into a disk about I inch thick and wrap with plastic wrap. Allow the dough to chill and rest for at least I hour in the refrigerator.

After the dough chills for 1 hour, unwrap it and roll it out evenly on a lightly floured surface into a 12-inch round. Drape the round over a 10-inch fluted tart pan with a removable bottom, and gently press the dough into the bottom and up the sides of the pan. Trim the top edge of the tart by running the rolling pin over the fluted edge of the pan. Refrigerate while you make the filling.

Preheat the oven to 350°F.

To make the walnut filling, stir together the flour, brown sugar, nutmeg, and cinnamon in a bowl and set aside. Over low heat, melt the butter in a small sauce-pan. Remove from the heat, add the flour mixture to the melted butter, and stir thoroughly. Add the corn syrup, beaten egg, and vanilla, mixing well into a smooth batter. Add the walnuts, mix thoroughly, and pour the mixture into the unbaked tart shell. Bake until the filling is firm to the touch and the crust is golden brown, 25 to 30 minutes. Remove from the oven and let cool on a wire rack. Serve warm or at room temperature.

SERVES **8** TO **10**

MENU

34 • Fish Roe Spread with Crostini (TARAMOSALATA)

35 • Classic Greek Roasted Chicken
with Lemon and Herbs (KOTOPOULO PSITO)

36 • Church-Style Lemon-Roasted Potatoes
(PATATES LEMONATES)

37 • Stewed Green Beans with Fresh Oregano
(FASSOULAKIA YAHNI)

38 • Milk Pie (GALATOBOUREKO)

ROASTING A CHICKEN WITH LEMON AND HERBS •
The Zouboukos brothers cook an old-fashioned church supper, Jackson style

If you've seen the movie *My Big Fat Greek Wedding,* you have an idea of what it's like growing up in a close-knit Greek community. When I was a girl in Jackson, Mississippi, we had what I called "Celebration Sundays." For any special occasion—a baptism, a wedding rehearsal dinner, Palm Sunday—almost every Greek in town would gather at the church hall to share the meal.

Our church was a tall brick building in the middle of a working-class neighborhood, but walk through the door and you suddenly stood in a completely different world: long dark wooden pews, deep red altar curtains, golden icons catching the light from dozens of candles along the walls.

If you were coming to the dinner, you'd walk quietly through the church and then, once you walked through the side door into the hall, you'd be met with all the noise of a church kitchen—pots clanging, kids playing, grown-ups laughing while they cooked together.

Pete and Jimmy Zouboukos, the owners of one of Jackson's best restaurants, the Elite, often led the charge for these "Celebration Sundays," cooking the entire meal in our church kitchen. I remember watching them cook twelve chickens at a time and stir big pans full of potatoes and green beans. Even as a kid, I noticed how Pete and Jimmy moved effortlessly between counter and stove, stepping between hordes of running kids without missing a beat, making great food in a crowded kitchen with few conveniences.

I loved the lemony chicken with its crisp skin and the smooth, rich custard of the pie, but for me, the highlight of the meal was always Pete's potatoes. The golden brown crust on his potatoes had an amazing buttery lemon flavor and they were incredibly tender inside. I think Pete used canned potatoes; I use only beautiful little Yukon golds with their unbeatable flavor, but I worry that my potatoes still fall slightly short of Pete's.

This meal seems to me a universal Sunday dinner. Lemon-roasted chicken with fresh herbs, buttery potatoes, tender green beans—with a few changes in seasonings you'd find this combination in New York and California, Europe and South America, and just about every place in between.

The recipes in this menu feed from four to six people. If I were cooking a real Pete and Jimmy–style church supper, I'd make enough to feed at least two hundred hungry Greek Southerners.

Anywhere Greeks gather together you'll find *salata*. When Greeks say salad, they're not referring just to lettuce and vegetables or fruit, the way we do when we say salad. In Greece, this blend of *tarama* (fish roe), lemon juice, fresh parsley, and garlic counts as a *salata*, too, even if it's rich and addictive. Many Greeks eat this daily, all year round, and they double their consumption during Lent.

Americans are just now developing a taste for fish roe, and this appetizing spread makes it very accessible. I love to spread this on crostini (the recipe follows), but it's also nice as a spread for breads, a dip for crackers, celery, or cucumber sticks, or just with pita bread. Often called "poor man's caviar," *taramosalata* is found in just about every taverna in Greece, where it's served with ouzo, the anise-flavored liqueur beloved by Greeks, or retsina wine, as well as at every church supper in Jackson.

I'll sometimes pack up a pita-bread picnic and take *taramosalata*, cucumber-yogurt *tzatziki* (page 58), Spicy Feta Spread (page 59), and Artichoke Hearts Braised in Lemon Juice (page 57). Set out with fresh rounds of pita bread, these four dishes make a wonderfully light but satisfying al fresco meal.

Taramosalata tastes best if you make it the day before and let the flavors meld. If you can't find carp roe sold near you, see the Resources section on page 190.

¹/₂ cup water

¹/₂ cup whole milk

Three 1-inch slices white bread, crusts removed

¹/₂ cup *tarama* (carp roe)

2 cups minced yellow onion

3 tablespoons fresh lemon juice

³/₄ cup extra-virgin olive oil

1 tablespoon finely chopped fresh Italian (flat-leaf) parsley

Crostini for serving (optional) (recipe follows)

Crostini

1 clove garlic, minced

2 tablespoons unsalted butter, at room temperature

12 slices crusty, rustic bread

1 teaspoon kosher salt

Fish Roe Spread with Crostini ✦
TARAMOSALATA

In a bowl, combine the water and milk. Soak the bread thoroughly in the milk mixture for 10 to 15 minutes. Squeeze the bread dry. Put the squeezed bread, the roe, onion, lemon juice, and olive oil in a blender or food processor and process until smooth. Its texture will be similar to hummus, and you should be able to spread it easily with a knife. If it's too thick, add water a teaspoon at a time until the desired consistency is reached.

Fold in the parsley and refrigerate overnight. Serve with the crostini, or grilled or toasted bread.

SERVES 6 GENEROUSLY

Crostini

Preheat the oven to 350°F.

In a small bowl, mix together the garlic and butter. Spread the mixture onto each slice of bread and sprinkle with salt. Arrange the slices on a baking sheet and bake until crisp and golden brown, about 10 minutes. If you're grilling, you may grill the slices instead of baking them.

MAKES 12 CROSTINI

You can't go wrong with a roasted chicken. When I first began cooking seriously, this was my specialty. This might be one of the most basic things you'll ever cook, but still there's something magical about putting a plain chicken in the oven and pulling out a golden brown, crisp-skinned bird, fragrant with herbs and lemon. The lemon juice brightens the flavor of the chicken and brings out the taste of the herbs. I'm partial to rosemary, but feel free to use a little creative license and substitute the fresh herbs you like best.

Classic Greek Roasted Chicken with Lemon and Herbs • KOTOPOULO PSITO

1 chicken (3 1/2 pounds), preferably free-range

1 tablespoon plus 1 1/2 teaspoons extra-virgin olive oil, plus extra for greasing

1 lemon, halved

1 teaspoon kosher salt

1/2 teaspoon freshly ground black pepper

1 tablespoon roughly chopped mixed herbs such as marjoram, rosemary, thyme, and sage

3 large cloves garlic, slightly broken

Preheat the oven to 400°F.

Remove the giblets and the neck from the body cavity of the chicken. (You can use these pieces to make stock for a quick gravy or other uses, or simply discard them.) Trim the tips of the wings and the skin at both ends of the bird. Rinse inside and outside, and pat dry with paper towels.

Rub the chicken on all sides with the olive oil, then squeeze the lemon over the chicken. Rub in the salt, pepper, and herb mixture on the outside of the chicken, and then place a pinch of each in the cavity along with the juiced halves of the lemon and the garlic.

Place in a lightly oiled roasting pan and roast, uncovered, until the juices run clear from a leg when pierced in the thickest part, about 45 minutes. Let the chicken rest for 10 minutes before carving.

SERVES 4

Fresh lemons are the secret ingredient behind the "church pota-toes" that Pete and Jimmy Zouboukos made every Sunday. The combination of fresh lemon juice and butter makes these little potatoes taste terrific. Cook them in a hot oven, and just keep pushing them around on the baking sheet until they're crispy all over and very tender inside. (While on Skopelos, I found another way to add lemon flavor to roasted potatoes—see my recipe for Skopelos-Style Grilled Potatoes on page 178.)

I like Yukon gold potatoes in this recipe, but Red Bliss or finger-ling potatoes work well, too.

Church-Style Lemon-Roasted Potatoes • PATATES LEMONATES

2 tablespoons extra-virgin olive oil

1 tablespoon unsalted butter

2 pounds small Yukon gold potatoes, peeled

$1/2$ cup fresh lemon juice

1 teaspoon finely chopped fresh thyme

$1/2$ teaspoon kosher salt

$1/4$ teaspoon freshly ground black pepper

Preheat the oven to 400°F.

In a 12-inch sauté pan, heat the olive oil and butter together over medium-high heat until the butter is golden brown. Add the potatoes and toss lightly so all sides are coated. Transfer to a baking sheet or baking dish. Bake until tender when pierced with a knife, about 30 minutes. (It's not necessary, but I like to turn the potatoes so they get brown on all sides.) Sprinkle with the lemon juice, thyme, salt, and pepper. Toss and serve hot.

SERVES **4** TO **6**

When I make this dish, I'm never sure if the Greeks influenced the Italians or the Italians influenced the Greeks. Either way, the sunny combination of tomatoes, garlic, and oregano brings out the best in these beans, and feta cheese sprinkled over the top somehow boosts the flavor of the beans and the herbs. See Resources on page 190 if you have trouble finding great feta.

Stewed Green Beans with Fresh Oregano • FASSOULAKIA YAHNI

¼ cup extra-virgin olive oil

2 cups chopped yellow onions

I clove garlic, finely chopped

One 14 ½-ounce can diced tomatoes with juice

I tablespoon finely chopped fresh Italian (flat-leaf) parsley

I teaspoon kosher salt

½ teaspoon freshly ground black pepper

I tablespoon finely chopped fresh oregano

I cup water

I pound fresh green beans, trimmed

¼ cup crumbled feta cheese for garnish (optional)

In a saucepan, heat the olive oil over medium heat. Add the onions and sauté until soft and clear, about 10 minutes. Add the garlic and cook briefly until soft and golden brown. Add the tomatoes with their juice, the parsley, salt, pepper, oregano, and water. Stir in the green beans and bring to a boil. Reduce the heat, cover, and let simmer until the beans are tender but still have a bit of crunch to them, about 12 minutes. Taste and adjust the seasoning.

Spoon onto a warm platter and top with the feta, if desired.

SERVES 4 TO 6

This dessert is much, much better than the name "milk pie" would lead you to believe. With crisp layers of phyllo dough and a rich vanilla custard, all topped with a hot lemon syrup, *galatoboureko* makes me think of crème brûlée gently wrapped in feather-light pastry.

Although baklava is Greece's best-known dessert beyond its borders, to Greeks *galatoboureko* is just as classic. This is my absolute favorite Greek dessert because I love the difference in textures. You begin the pie with layers of phyllo dough, lay in the custard, top with more phyllo, and bake the pie. The second it comes out of the oven, you pour over cooled lemon syrup that adds another layer of texture on top of the crisp phyllo and soft custard. This recipe is easier than it sounds and well worth the effort.

See "Tips for Handling Phyllo Dough," facing page, before you begin this recipe.

Milk Pie ⋄ GALATOBOUREKO

4 cups whole milk

¹/₂ cup fine semolina flour

I cup sugar

10 tablespoons unsalted butter, melted, plus extra for greasing

4 large eggs

¹/₂ teaspoon vanilla extract

I pound phyllo dough (20 sheets)

Syrup

3 cups water

2 cups sugar

¹/₂ large lemon

In a large, heavy saucepan, bring the milk to a boil, then reduce the heat to low. Sprinkle in the semolina, whisking steadily. Add the sugar and simmer for 5 to 6 minutes, stirring occasionally. Remove from the heat and whisk in half of the melted butter. Add the eggs, one at a time, stirring well after each addition. Stir in the vanilla. The mixture will be thick but pourable, like a soft polenta. Set aside.

Preheat the oven to 375°F.

Butter a 9-by-13-inch baking dish. Line the bottom of the dish with 8 of the phyllo sheets, layering them one at a time, gently smoothing each sheet and brushing it with some of the remaining melted butter before adding the next sheet. Gently press the phyllo into the corners of the dish, allowing any excess to come up the sides. Keep the stack of phyllo you're not working with covered with a damp kitchen towel.

Smooth the top sheet of phyllo and brush with butter. Pour the filling over the top. Cover with the remaining 12 sheets of phyllo dough, again gently smoothing and brushing each sheet with butter before adding another. Brush the top with butter and trim the dough around the edges of the dish with a knife or scissors. With a very sharp knife, score the top in two directions to form diamond-shaped pieces, taking care not to cut more than the first layer or two of phyllo. Sprinkle the top with a little water and bake until the top is golden brown and the filling is set, 45 minutes to I hour.

As soon as you put the pie in the oven, make the syrup. Combine the water and sugar in a heavy saucepan. Squeeze the lemon into the sugared water, then drop the juiced half in the liquid. Simmer over low heat for about 45 minutes. Remove from the heat and discard the lemon. Let the syrup cool and then pour over the pie as soon as you take it from the oven.

Let the pie cool completely, then cut along the score lines and serve.

SERVES 18

Tips for Handling Phyllo Dough

Even in Skopelos, most people no longer make their own phyllo dough. If you visit Greece, find a phyllo dough shop and watch as a small round of dough is transformed into a four-foot-long pliable sheet no thicker than a piece of paper. It's miraculous. The phyllo maker cuts these sheets precisely and lays them in boxes, to be picked up throughout the morning by Greeks who appreciate the art behind perfect phyllo but are happy not to make it from scratch.

Here in the United States, phyllo comes from the grocer's freezer. The recipes in this book assume a standard package: A 1-pound box contains about twenty 14-by-18-inch sheets. Thawed phyllo is very fragile, without the elasticity of the fresh-made phyllo in Greece. Follow these tips, and don't get too caught up in making each layer perfect.

- Take the package of phyllo dough from the freezer the night before you plan to use it and let it thaw in your refrigerator.

- Dried phyllo will crack. To keep it whole, take the stack of phyllo from the box, place on a dry countertop, and cover with a slightly damp kitchen towel. As soon as you take one sheet from the pile, re-cover the rest with the towel to keep in moisture.

- If possible, the bottom and top layer of phyllo in the dish should be a solid piece. Subsequent layers can be "pieced together" without affecting your *spanakopita* or baklava. (I know this for a fact because my mom is the queen of piecing phyllo.) If the sheet tears or cracks, set it aside, and use another whole piece for the bottom.

- If your phyllo sheets are larger than the baking pan, press the sheets gently into the corners, making sure the bottom of the pan is evenly covered with the phyllo dough. Don't worry about the excess dough coming up the sides of the pan. When you've finished assembling a *galatoboureko, spanakopita,* or other assembled dish, trim the edges with a very sharp knife or scissors so no phyllo dough extends above the pan, where it could burn.

MENU

42 • Pork Skewers with Pita Bread
(SOUVLAKI ME PITA)

43 • Spiro's Brisket (VODINO SPIROS)

45 • Greek Potato Salad
(PATATOSALATA)

46 • Bell Peppers Stuffed with Meat and Rice
(PIPERIES YEMISTES ME KIMA KAI RIZI)

48 • Greek Butter Cookies
(KOURAMBIEDES)

SLOW-SMOKING A BEEF BRISKET · Greek flavors take on a Southern flair when my dad cooks

My dad, Spiro Cora, is a natural-born brisket smoker. He can take a pretty hefty piece of beef and slow-smoke it until you can't imagine anything tasting better. He knows the best way to soak his hickory chips, when to add them to the barbecue, how to make the most of a fire. Plus, he's the calmest cook I know. In my earliest memories of my dad cooking, he's sitting beside his fire, checking the smoke occasionally and happily reading a book. No matter how hectic my surroundings, if I want to lower my blood pressure by ten points I just envision my father smoking a brisket.

Once friends and neighbors caught on to how good my dad's briskets were, we almost always had guests when he was cooking one. (I think the fragrant smoke drifting over our backyard fence was just about impossible to resist.) My mom learned to make lots of hearty dishes on brisket days so everybody around her table left satisfied no matter how many people pulled up a chair.

Beef brisket and the Greek potato salad *patatosalata* go together perfectly. A lemon-dill vinaigrette and Kalamata olives spark up the flavor of the tender red potatoes. This version is wonderful hot or cold, so you can make it ahead of time if you like.

Nobody stuffs vegetables like a Greek, and my dad is the master. Sweet bell peppers filled with a savory mix of meat, rice, cinnamon, and fresh mint satisfy on just about every level—enticing color, wonderful fragrance, and a great, robust flavor. You can make them with ground lamb, ground beef, or a combination.

While I was growing up, cookies were a given—they were almost always available as an easy dessert or after-school snack. The Greek butter cookies *kourambiedes* have very little sugar in their dough. The sweetness comes from the confectioners' sugar that you dip them in while they're still warm. My mom always adds a small indentation to each cookie just before baking, creating a dimple to hold a little extra sugar. She says this is to hold in a bit more of life's sweetness—or to tempt my dad to grab a cookie before the Easter fast was over.

For most families, these pork skewers would be the center of a meal; for my family, these juicy, grilled chunks of pork are just a starter. On Skopelos, for Easter dinner—the biggest meal of the year—my uncle Yiorgios slides these succulent pieces of pork on heavy four-foot-long metal skewers. These roast over the fire on either side of the goat, and when they're done, my uncle pulls the skewers off the fire, pushes the sizzling meat onto a huge platter, and serves the pork right away to tide us over until the goat's done.

Fresh lemon juice is key. For pork that's juicy, tender, and flavorful, marinate overnight in this fragrant blend of lemon, olive oil, garlic, and herbs.

Pork Skewers with Pita Bread •
SOUVLAKI ME PITA

2 pounds boneless pork shoulder, cut into 1 1/2-inch cubes

1/2 cup fresh lemon juice

3 tablespoons extra-virgin olive oil, plus 1/2 cup

6 cloves garlic, minced

2 tablespoons finely chopped fresh oregano, plus 1 teaspoon

1 tablespoon finely chopped fresh thyme

1/2 teaspoon kosher salt, plus more to taste

1/4 teaspoon freshly ground black pepper, plus more to taste

Six 8-inch metal or wooden skewers

3 cups shredded green-leaf lettuce

1 small white onion, halved and thinly sliced into half moons

3 large tomatoes, diced

3 tablespoons red wine vinegar

6 halved and split rounds of pita bread

In a bowl, toss together the pork, lemon juice, the 3 tablespoons olive oil, the garlic, 2 tablespoons oregano, the thyme, 1/2 teaspoon salt, and 1/4 teaspoon pepper. Cover and refrigerate for at least 3 hours or for up to 24 hours.

Before you're ready to cook, if you're using wooden skewers, soak them in a shallow pan of warm water for at least 1 hour before sliding on the meat. Prepare a fire in a charcoal grill or preheat a gas grill to high.

Toss together the lettuce, onion slices, tomatoes, the 1/2 cup olive oil, the vinegar, and the 1 teaspoon oregano in a bowl. Season with salt and pepper to taste and set aside.

Thread each of the skewers with the marinated pork. Place the skewers on an area of the grill with no direct flame. Grill, turning as needed and brushing with marinade every few minutes, until the meat is cooked through and browned to suit your taste.

Serve immediately in the pita pockets, topped with the salad.

SERVES 6

This cut of meat, cooked the way my father makes it, just might be my brother Mike's favorite food. Whenever my dad smokes a brisket (see page 44), you usually can find Mike nearby. He loves the flavor of this beef hot off the grill as well as cold the next day in sandwiches.

My dad's seasonings for his beef are so simple—and yet I'm always surprised when I take that first bite by how good an inexpensive cut of meat can taste.

My dad uses this same marinade for chicken and lamb, too. He sometimes squeezes in the juice of a third lemon because he likes his meat to have an extra-citrusy zing. You can marinate the beef for as little as 30 minutes, but you get a lot more flavor when you marinate overnight.

Spiro's Brisket • VODINO SPIROS

1 beef brisket (3 pounds)

Juice of 2 lemons

$1/_4$ cup Worcestershire sauce

6 cloves garlic, finely chopped

2 teaspoons freshly ground black pepper

$1/_4$ cup finely chopped fresh oregano

Prepare a fire in a charcoal grill, or preheat a smoker or gas grill to low.

Place the brisket in a baking dish and pour the lemon juice and Worcestershire sauce over it. Turn it once to coat. Rub the garlic, pepper, and oregano on both sides. Let marinate for at least 30 minutes or up to 24 hours.

Place the brisket on an area of the grill with no direct flame and cook, without turning, until well done, about 2 hours.

SERVES 4 TO 6

Spiro's Tips for Smoking a Brisket

Follow my dad's tips for smoking and you'll have wonderfully tender, flavorful beef.

- Get two or three blocks of hickory and soak them for 36 to 48 hours. The fire will get very hot and you want to be sure the soaked wood doesn't burn. If your hickory is green, that's even better. You'll need to soak it for only about 24 hours. (You can drain the wood for a few minutes before you place it on the fire, but keep in mind that the wood needs to be moist to create smoke.)

- Inside a barrel smoker, heap hickory charcoal and blocks of hickory at one end, and place a disposable roasting pan filled with water at the other end. Start your fire.

- When the charcoal is gray, place your brisket in the smoker but over the pan of water rather than over the fire. If you like, set up a little barrier of aluminum foil to protect your brisket from flames.

- Close up the smoker and let the meat cook slowly for 2 hours for a small brisket and 4 to 6 hours for a medium to large brisket.

- To tell when your meat is ready, cheat: Cut off a little piece of meat to make sure it's well done. You don't want to serve a brisket rare. Cook it all the way through or, as my dad would say, "It'll be as tough as a piece of shoe leather."

Fine red potatoes, red onions, and scallions, dressed in a lemony vinaigrette with fresh dill and oregano—this is potato salad at its best. Kalamata olives and a hint of red wine vinegar spark the flavors perfectly. This crowd-pleaser is the salad to pack for picnics because it tastes wonderful cold or at room temperature.

I like Red Bliss potatoes, but you can make this salad with many varieties of red-skinned potatoes and have good results.

Greek Potato Salad • PATATOSALATA

2 pounds red potatoes (about 20 medium potatoes), scrubbed but unpeeled

1 $^{3}/_{4}$ teaspoons kosher salt

1 medium red onion, halved and sliced into half moons

$^{1}/_{4}$ cup thinly chopped scallions (about 2 scallions) white and tender green parts

24 Kalamata olives, pitted and halved

1 tablespoon finely chopped fresh dill

1 tablespoon finely chopped fresh oregano

$^{1}/_{4}$ cup extra-virgin olive oil

1 tablespoon red wine vinegar

$^{1}/_{4}$ cup fresh lemon juice

$^{1}/_{4}$ teaspoon freshly ground black pepper

Place the potatoes in a large saucepan with cold water to cover. Add 1 teaspoon of the salt and bring to a rolling boil over high heat. Reduce the heat to medium and simmer until the potatoes are tender when pierced with a knife, 20 to 25 minutes.

While the potatoes are cooking, combine the red onion slices, scallions, olives, dill, and oregano in a salad bowl and set aside. When the potatoes are done, drain well in a colander and allow to cool slightly. Cut the potatoes into quarters and add them to the salad bowl.

In a small bowl, whisk together the olive oil, vinegar, lemon juice, remaining $^{3}/_{4}$ teaspoon salt, and pepper. Pour over the salad and mix well. Taste and adjust the seasoning. Serve warm or refrigerate until ready to serve.

SERVES **4** TO **6**

Because meat was at one time hard to come by on the islands, Greeks have learned to create dishes that give you a taste of meat with equal portions of rice and vegetables. Stuffed vegetables are a perfect example. The Greeks excel at stuffed vegetables, and my dad is the best in the house. He likes to add just a touch of cinnamon to his stuffing for a little extra savoriness.

You have some creative license with this dish. Use green, red, or yellow bell peppers, or even some of the wilder colors now available—bright purple or orange. A combination of colors makes for a great presentation. My dad fills his peppers with lamb, but you can use just ground beef or a combination of beef and lamb, which I like because it makes this dish a little more robust.

1/4 cup olive oil

1 large yellow onion, finely chopped

2 cloves garlic, minced

1/2 cup finely chopped celery

1 pound ground beef or lamb, or a combination of beef and lamb

One 28-ounce can tomatoes with juice (or one 6-ounce can tomato paste mixed with 3/4 cup water)

2 tablespoons finely chopped fresh mint (optional)

1 tablespoon finely chopped fresh oregano

1 teaspoon ground cinnamon

1 teaspoon kosher salt

1/2 teaspoon freshly ground black pepper

1 cup uncooked long-grain white rice

6 medium sweet bell peppers

Bell Peppers Stuffed with Meat and Rice
✦ PIPERIES YEMISTES ME KIMA KAI RIZI

In a large sauté pan, heat the olive oil over medium-high heat. Add the onion, garlic, and celery and cook until the onion is soft and clear, 3 to 4 minutes. Add the ground meat and brown lightly. Skim the excess fat. Dice the tomatoes and add both the tomatoes and their juice (or tomato paste and water) to the meat. Add the herbs, cinnamon, salt, and pepper and simmer for 5 minutes. Taste and adjust the seasoning. Add the rice and simmer until almost all the liquid has been absorbed, 10 to 15 minutes.

Preheat the oven to 350°F.

While the rice and meat mixture is simmering, slice off enough of the stem end of each bell pepper to expose the whole cavity. Reserve the tops. Remove the seeds and ribs from the pepper cavities and rinse with water. Use a spoon to fill each pepper loosely with the meat mixture, leaving room for the filling to expand. Replace the tops. Place the stuffed peppers in a 9-by-13-inch baking dish and pour in water to a depth of about 1/2 inch. Bake, basting every 15 minutes, until the rice in the filling is tender, about 1 hour. (Add more water if the dish becomes dry, and cover the peppers with aluminum foil if they begin to turn brown.) Serve immediately.

SERVES 6

Cookies were a big part of my upbringing, and these cookies, flavored with lemon, almonds, and cinnamon with a hint of cognac, were a family favorite.

Made with little sugar in the dough, these cookies are coated with confectioners' sugar as soon as you take them from the oven. My mom always added a dimple to the top of each cookie to hold a little extra sugar.

What's nice about these buttery cookies is how well they keep. The confectioners' sugar coats them, keeping the cookies soft and fresh. Store them in cookie jars or tins and they'll last for several weeks—if you can keep them hidden from the other cookie lovers in your house.

Greek Butter Cookies • KOURAMBIEDES

2 ¹/₂ cups unsalted butter, at room temperature

¹/₂ cup confectioners' sugar

2 egg yolks

2 tablespoons fresh lemon or orange juice

¹/₄ teaspoon baking soda

1 teaspoon vanilla extract

3 tablespoons cognac, brandy, or whiskey

1 cup almonds, toasted (see note, page 30) and coarsely ground

6 cups all-purpose flour

About 2 pounds confectioners' sugar

Ground cinnamon or cloves for dusting

Preheat the oven to 350°F. Line a baking sheet with parchment paper.

To make the dough, in the bowl of a stand mixer fitted with the paddle attachment, beat the butter until it is very light in color and fluffy, 12 to 15 minutes. Add the confectioners' sugar and continue to beat well. Add the egg yolks, one at a time, beating well after each addition.

In a small bowl, combine the lemon juice and baking soda. Mix gently and add the foaming mixture to the butter mixture, along with the vanilla and cognac. Mix well to incorporate the ingredients thoroughly.

Put the cooled, toasted almonds in a food processor with 1 cup of the flour and pulse until the mixture is the consistency of a coarse meal. (Don't overmix or you'll have nut butter!) Add the nut mixture and the remaining 5 cups flour to the butter mixture and mix slowly, thoroughly incorporating all of the dry ingredients to make a firm dough. If the dough is very soft, cover and refrigerate for about 1 hour to chill and firm before shaping the cookies.

Scoop up tablespoons of the dough and roll into balls, or, if desired, shape into crescents (the traditional shape in Greece), triangles, or stars. Place the cookies about

I inch apart on the prepared baking sheet. Press your finger lightly into each cookie to dimple the top. Bake until light golden brown, about 20 minutes. Repeat with the remaining dough.

While the cookies are baking, prepare a deep cookie jar, tin, or container by lining it with waxed paper and filling it with confectioners' sugar to a depth of I inch. (If you use shallow tins, have three or four ready.) When the cookies are done, remove from the oven and sprinkle each very lightly with cinnamon. Gently place the warm cookies in the prepared container and cover them completely with more confectioners' sugar. Alternate layers of cookies and sugar until the container is full. Let the cookies cool for at least 30 minutes before removing from the sugar and serving. (I like to save this sugar, sealing it tightly in a plastic bag, for my next batch of *kourambiedes*.)

If desired, place each cookie in a fluted paper liner or bonbon cup for serving. These cookies keep well for several weeks.

MAKES **5** TO **6** DOZEN COOKIES

The Karagiozos Kitchen on
SKOPELOS, GREECE

On Skopelos, on a hillside overlooking the sea, sits my grandfather's house. My entire family refers to it as "grandfather's house" even though Karagiozos have lived on this hill for centuries before my grandfather was born. The house is modest, but the table right outside the front door is huge. Every time I've sat at this table, surrounded by aunts, uncles, and cousins, we've shared enormous platters of lamb and huge loaves of bread cooked in their outdoor oven, olives and feta grown and made right on the island, and plates full of *horiatiki*, *htipiti*, and *spanakopita*.

When I first visited Skopelos after college, I reveled in the flavors of Greek food but never considered cooking it myself. When I returned to the island a decade later as a chef, it hit me like a bolt of lightning: Every food on my aunt's table was simple, authentic, and perfectly delicious— and each had a place in my family's history. I belong to a line of people that stretches back hundreds of years, all of them sitting under these trees, tasting these same flavors; all crowded around a table with a view of the sea. Suddenly, it seemed as though my years of training to be a chef had brought me here, back to this table, to learn how to bring these flavors home.

The recipes in this section span cultures and generations. I watched my Aunt Demetra and my great-aunt Eleni make these foods on Skopelos, then came home to the States and re-created them in my own kitchen. I altered a few of these recipes slightly to work with the modern appliances in American home kitchens but tried to keep them as authentically *Skopeletti* as possible.

MENU

55 • Spinach, Dill, and Feta Baked
in Phyllo Dough (SPANAKOPITA)

57 • Artichoke Hearts Braised
in Lemon Juice (ANGINARES ME LATHOLEMONO)

58 • Cucumber Yogurt (TZATZIKI)

59 • Spicy Feta Spread (HTIPITI)

61 • Sour Cherry Torte
(TORTES ME VISSINO GLYKO)

ARRIVING IN SKOPELOS • Aunt Demetra is worried we'll be hungry

Thirteen miles long and only five miles wide, Skopelos is a drumstick-shaped island in the Aegean Sea between Skiathos and Alonnisos. Skopelos has no airport, so you arrive by boat, the steep hills rising above you on three sides as the ferry chugs into port. It takes a few minutes to dock the boat, giving you time to take it all in, to notice how white the buildings in town look beside the green hills, and to see how steeply the streets wind up the hills dotted with olive, orange, and lemon trees. When I arrived for my first visit in ten years, I could see my uncle Yiorgios (pronounced "Yore-Go") and my cousin Yanni waiting on the dock. After warm greetings, we piled into the car and headed for the family home, where my Aunt Demetra had a meal warm and waiting.

Platters filled Demetra's table from end to end—bread she'd baked herself; bowls of lemon-braised artichokes and a spicy, lemony feta spread; a slab of fresh feta cheese; and, best of all, a warm, golden brown *spanakopita*, which filled the room with the fragrance of fresh dill and parsley.

Demetra cut into the *spanakopita*, and watched as I took my first taste. Crisp, light layers of phyllo surrounded the lush, tender filling of fresh spinach, dill, and feta cheese.

I struggled to tell her how much the meal meant to me. Demetra speaks little English and I speak a limited amount of Greek, but when she came around the table to hug me I knew she understood when I said that this food and the family around this table had brought me back to Greece.

You'll be amazed by how much fresh spinach goes into this *spanakopita*. Choose spinach with bright, full leaves because that's the flavor underlying the fresh dill, fresh parsley, and feta cheese.

The feta is the other flavor you'll want to choose with care. I think French feta cheeses are too mild—and don't even get me started on Danish fetas, which are made with cow's milk and taste altogether different from Greek feta. Go to a cheese market and taste Greek fetas. Choose a feta with some flavor; a delicate cheese will be lost beneath the spinach and dill. If you can't find a feta you really like, see the Resources on page 190.

Rice in a *spanakopita* is somewhat unusual, but just a little rice, toasted lightly in olive oil, adds wonderful texture to the filling.

Don't hesitate to make this even if you're cooking just for two or four people. It keeps well refrigerated for several days, and actually packs up nicely for brown-bag lunches.

See "Tips for Handling Phyllo Dough" on page 39 before you begin this recipe.

Spinach, Dill, and Feta Baked in Phyllo Dough • SPANAKOPITA

$1/2$ cup extra-virgin olive oil, plus extra for greasing and brushing

6 cups chopped yellow onions

$3/4$ cup uncooked long-grain white rice

$4 1/2$ pounds fresh spinach, tough stems removed

$2 1/4$ teaspoons kosher salt

3 scallions, white and tender green parts, chopped

$3/4$ cup finely chopped fresh Italian (flat-leaf) parsley

$1/4$ cup plus 2 tablespoons finely chopped fresh dill

$1 1/2$ cups crumbled feta cheese

$1/2$ teaspoon freshly ground black pepper

1 pound phyllo dough (20–24 sheets)

Preheat the oven to 350°F.

Heat the $1/2$ cup olive oil in a stockpot over medium-high heat. Add the onions and sauté until lightly browned. Add the rice and stir until each grain is coated with oil, 2 to 3 minutes. Add the spinach in 5 small batches, folding the raw leaves under with a spoon as you add each batch. With each of the first 4 batches of spinach, add $1/2$ teaspoon salt; add $1/4$ teaspoon salt with the fifth and final batch. Allow each batch to wilt down before you add more spinach.

When all of the spinach is wilted, stir in the scallions, parsley, and dill. Strain off the liquid from the pot and let the spinach mixture cool. (If you spread it out on a baking sheet, it will cool faster.) Once the mixture is cool, add the feta and pepper.

Brush a 9-by-13-by-2-inch baking dish with olive oil. Line the bottom of the dish with half of the phyllo sheets (10 to 12 sheets), layering them one at a time; press smooth, gently pressing the dough into the corners of the dish, and brush each

continued

sheet with olive oil before adding the next sheet. Allow any excess to come up the sides of the dish. Keep the stack of phyllo you're not working with covered with a damp kitchen towel.

Smooth the top sheet of phyllo and brush with olive oil. Spread the spinach filling evenly over the top. Cover with the remaining sheets of phyllo, again gently smoothing and brushing each sheet with olive oil before adding another. Brush the top with olive oil and trim the dough around the edges of the dish with a knife or scissors. With a very sharp knife, score the top into 12 squares, taking care not to cut more than the top layer or two of phyllo. Bake until the top is golden brown, about 40 minutes. Let cool, then cut along the score lines and serve.

SERVES 12

These artichokes are some of the best I've ever tasted. The bulb is cleaned down to the heart, leaving just a hint of stem, and then slow-braised in white wine and lemon juice seasoned with garlic and fresh thyme. Serve this dish warm or chilled with crackers and antipasti, salads, a pasta of wild mushrooms, or grilled fish.

Fresh lemon juice is the key ingredient when you're preparing artichoke hearts. If you pop the artichoke hearts into the lemon juice mixture as soon as you've trimmed them, you'll prevent the hearts from oxidizing, which turns them brown.

Artichoke Hearts Braised in Lemon Juice
◆ ANGINARES ME LATHOLEMONO

$1/2$ cup extra-virgin olive oil

$1/2$ cup fresh lemon juice

$1/4$ cup dry white wine

2 tablespoons chopped fresh thyme leaves or 2 teaspoons dried thyme

1 tablespoon kosher salt

1 teaspoon freshly ground black pepper

3 cloves garlic, minced

1 bay leaf

10 large artichokes

2 lemons, halved

Preheat the oven to 350°F.

In a Dutch oven or flameproof roasting pan, combine all the ingredients except the artichokes and lemon halves.

Working with 1 artichoke at a time, pull off and discard the small bottom leaves. Snap off the thick outer leaves by bending them back and pulling them down toward the stem; the meaty lower section of each leaf should remain anchored to the heart of the artichoke. Continue removing the leaves until those remaining are tender and yellow. Cut off about two-thirds of the tops of the remaining leaves (to where the meaty part of the heart begins) then cut off the stem where it meets the base. Trim around the base of the artichoke heart to smooth the sides and remove any dark green leaves that are not tender. Scoop out the fuzzy choke with a small spoon. Squeeze lemon juice over the heart and add to the pan with the braising liquid. Repeat with the remaining artichokes, spooning the braising liquid over the other hearts in the pan each time you complete an artichoke.

Bring the artichokes and liquid to a boil on top of the stove. Cover the pot with a lid or aluminum foil and transfer to the oven. Braise until the hearts are tender when pierced with a knife, 30 to 45 minutes.

Remove the pan from the oven, uncover, and let the artichokes cool in the braising liquid. Serve warm, or refrigerate and serve chilled. The artichokes will keep, refrigerated in their liquid in a container with a tight-fitting lid, for up to 3 weeks.

SERVES **4** TO **6**

This cool, tangy yogurt takes just minutes to make, and yet it's so delicious on so many foods, it makes its way to my table on a regular basis. Add a little diced red onion and try this as a wholesome substitute for mayonnaise in tuna or chicken salads. My family in Greece treats this as a condiment, and prepares it just about daily to serve with roasted chicken, brisket, pita bread, meatballs, and fried fish. It's considered essential with roasted lamb; even the *gyros* vendors on the streets in Athens won't let you walk away without a dollop of *tzatziki* on top of the meat.

There are a dozen different ways to cut cucumber for *tzatziki*—sliced, chunky, minced, diced—but my favorite method is the one I learned while on Skopelos. Using an old-fashioned metal grater, I grate my peeled cucumber right up to the seeds while holding it over the yogurt to catch all the juices and the flavor.

Cucumber Yogurt • TZATZIKI

I tablespoon fresh lemon juice

$^1\!/_2$ cup extra-virgin olive oil

I clove garlic, minced

I teaspoon kosher salt

2 cups plain yogurt (regular or low-fat)

I medium cucumber, peeled and halved lengthwise

In a bowl, combine the lemon juice, olive oil, garlic, salt, and yogurt. Grate the cucumber halves into the yogurt mixture up to the seeds; discard the seeds. Mix well. Refrigerate for at least I hour. Serve chilled.

SERVES **4** TO **6**

I adore feta, and am happy with a big chunk of it and a glass of red wine. This spicy, lemony spread is a more elegant way to show off feta's hearty flavor. Spread *htipiti* on grilled country bread for a Greek-style bruschetta or serve as a dip with toasted pita or crackers. Try this spread on toasted slices of *eliopita* (page 102), a hearty quick bread made with lots of Kalamata olives.

Be sure to use a robust, full-bodied Greek feta for this recipe. If you have trouble finding a terrific feta, see Resources on page 190.

Spicy Feta Spread • HTIPITI

In a food processor or blender, combine the feta, olive oil, peperoncini, red pepper flakes, garlic, oregano, and black pepper. Process on low speed until the mixture has a whipped consistency, 3 to 4 minutes.

Add the lemon juice and pulse until completely combined. Spoon into a bowl, cover, and refrigerate for at least 1 hour or until ready to use. Serve chilled, with toasted pita, crackers, or bread.

SERVES **4** TO **6**

1 $^1/_2$ cups crumbled feta cheese

2 tablespoons extra-virgin olive oil

1 teaspoon finely chopped peperoncini peppers

$^1/_2$ teaspoon red pepper flakes

1 clove garlic, minced

1 teaspoon finely chopped fresh oregano

$^1/_8$ teaspoon freshly ground black pepper

1 tablespoon fresh lemon juice

Toasted pita, baguette slices, or crackers for serving

Filling

Two 14 1/2-ounce cans sour cherries, juice reserved

4 cups sugar

Juice of 1 lemon (zest reserved)

Dough

1 cup unsalted butter, at room temperature

2 cups all-purpose flour

1 teaspoon baking soda

1/2 teaspoon salt

1/2 cup sugar

1 egg

1 teaspoon vanilla extract

2 teaspoons lemon zest (above; see page 22)

Note: This recipe requires a bit more technical proficiency than the other recipes in this section. Sour cherries are notoriously tricky to cook into syrup. In Greece, where home cooks often make their preserves without the help of a thermometer, it's common for the syrup to stubbornly refuse to thicken. In Greek villages, a common way to say "What's the matter?" is "Den sou edese to vissino?" Literally translated, this means, "Did your preserves not thicken?"

If you're comfortable working with a jelly or candy thermometer, this recipe is just your speed.

In Greece, *vissino glyko*, or sour cherry preserves, aren't just spread on toast the way we serve jams and jellies here in the United States. They're set out in tiny dishes, often a family's most prized crystal or china, to show off the preserves' beautiful color. Guests eat them plain, with tiny spoons, which gives them their name, "spoon sweets."

There's a whole ritual to serving spoon sweets in Greece. Here in the States, if you set a spoonful of sour cherry preserves in perfect tiny dishes in front of your guests, they'd be baffled. *Vissino glyko* is such a strong part of the culture in Greece, I couldn't bear to leave sour cherries out of this book, so I created a recipe for a torte with the help of my mom, Virginia Cora. Made in the style of a European *torten*, this cakelike dough is just the right complement to the flavor of sour cherries.

Sour Cherry Torte ·

TORTES ME VISSINO GLYKO

To make the filling, strain the cherries, reserving their juice, and set aside the cherries in a separate bowl. Pour 1 cup of the cherry juice into a saucepan. Add the sugar, place over low heat, and stir gently until the sugar is completely dissolved. Raise the heat to medium-low and continue to stir while the mixture comes to a slow simmer. Skim any foam that forms. Simmer the syrup gently for 10 minutes, or until it reaches 220°F on a candy or jelly thermometer.

Add the cherries and lemon juice to the syrup and cook gently over low heat for 10 to 15 minutes, allowing the mixture to thicken. You don't want the syrup to caramelize, so keep the temperature just below 223°F. The syrup should be bright red, moderately thick, and clinging to the fruit, but take care not to overcook. Remove from the heat and let the syrup and cherries cool to room temperature. (If you like, to test the thickness of the syrup, pour a tablespoon or two onto a small plate and place in the refrigerator. Chill for 15 minutes. Remove from the refrigerator. The syrup should be thick, not runny, with a deep red color. If the syrup seems thin, return to 220°F and cook for another 3 to 5 minutes.) Transfer the cherries and syrup to a covered container and refrigerate for several hours or overnight, allowing the cherries to absorb the syrup and to become plump.

To make the dough, in the bowl of a stand mixer fitted with the paddle attachment, beat the butter at medium-high speed until it is light in color and fluffy, 5 to 7 minutes. Meanwhile, sift together the flour, baking soda, and salt into a separate bowl. Set aside. Add the sugar to the creamed butter and mix thoroughly. One at a time, add the egg, vanilla, and 1 teaspoon of the lemon zest, thoroughly incorporating each addition. Slowly add the sifted dry ingredients, blending them into the butter mixture thoroughly without overworking the dough.

continued

Scoop the soft dough onto a piece of plastic wrap, covering the dough loosely but completely. With a rolling pin, roll the dough into a round disk. (The plastic wrap will be tight around the dough.) Let the dough rest in the refrigerator for I hour or more.

When the dough is firm to the touch, unwrap it and roll it out evenly on a lightly floured surface into a 12-inch round. Drape the round over a 10-inch fluted tart pan with a removable bottom and gently press the dough into the bottom and up the sides of the pan. Trim the top edge of the tart by running a rolling pin over the fluted edge of the pan. (You can fill the tart shell with the cherry mixture and bake it right away, or cover the unfilled, unbaked shell and refrigerate until you're ready to add the cherry mixture and bake your torte.)

Preheat the oven to 350°F.

Pour the cherries and syrup into a strainer set over a large bowl, allowing most of the syrup to separate from the fruit. Pour the cherries with the syrup clinging to them into the unbaked tart shell, spreading them evenly over the entire surface. Sprinkle the remaining I teaspoon lemon zest evenly over the cherries. Add 3 or 4 tablespoons of the fruit syrup, spreading it evenly over the cherries; the shell should be barely half full. Store the remaining syrup in the refrigerator.

Bake until the torte is light golden brown around the edges, 15 to 20 minutes. Remove from the oven and transfer to a wire rack to cool. Serve at room temperature.

SERVES **6** TO **8**

MENU

67 • Stewed Rabbit with Pearl Onions
(KOUNELI STIFATHO)

70 • Polenta with Fontina and Parmesan

71 • Fresh Spinach with Preserved Lemons
(SPANAKI ME LEMONE)

72 • Honey-Dipped Cookies with Fresh Figs
(MELOMAKARONA KAI SIKA)

COOKING A CLASSIC *STIFATHO* WITH MY AUNT
DEMETRA • This Greek stew calls for rabbit, wine, and beautiful pearl onions

If there's one dish that's a constant throughout Greece, it's *stifatho,* or stew made with beautiful little pearl onions, ripe, juicy tomatoes, and fresh thyme and oregano. A *stifatho* can be made of beef, chicken, or even fish, but traditional *stifatho* is made with rabbit, which Greeks have hunted on the hillsides near their villages for thousands of years. The combination of red wine and red wine vinegar adds depth to the stew while bringing out the rabbit's flavor.

Without a doubt, red pearl onions give a *stifatho* a more authentic flavor. Red pearl onions aren't easy to find in the United States, so if people ask me, I tell them, "If you can't find red pearl onions, substitute white pearl onions." Of course, every time I say this, I seem to turn around to find a Greek who's overheard me, shaking his or her head sadly. By all means, try to find red pearl onions (and check Resources on page 190), but if you don't have red pearl onions and do have nice white pearl onions, your *stifatho* will still be very, very good.

Polenta isn't traditionally Greek, but it's a natural with *stifatho* or, for my money, anything with sauce. With my polenta, I add both fontina and Parmesan cheese for a sophisticated flavor.

Greens, for me, are the country version of a palate cleanser. Speaking for myself, I'd much rather have a plate of juicy, bright green spinach than a sorbet between courses. This spinach, with the flavor of preserved lemons, is just the right texture and flavor beside the *stifatho* and polenta—but it's also perfect all by itself as a very light meal late at night, when you want something homey yet wholesome. I keep preserved lemons on hand for this very purpose.

A meal this hearty calls for something light afterward. When you pour coffee after the meal, move the party to the living room and bring out a plate of deep, dark spice cookies with a plate of fresh Black Mission figs, the most grown-up cookies I know alongside the most grown-up fruit.

When I first prepared rabbit, I quickly realized it's very much like cooking a chicken, except the flavor is better. Don't be intimidated by rabbit. You can ask your butcher to cut it for you; a good butcher will be happy to help, and once the rabbit is cut, cooking it is no harder than cooking chicken.

Stifatho, or stew, may be the oldest cooking method in Greece. Every island has its own version of *stifatho* for beef, for pork, for chicken or rabbit, and even for fish. This *stifatho* starts with rabbit and pearl onions; red wine and red wine vinegar have been my family's secret for rich, tender meat in a hearty, savory stew.

You can substitute white pearl onions if there are no Greeks watching you cook. If you manage to find red pearl onions, please bring them home and make this stew—they bring an inimitable flavor and sweetness to the *stifatho*. (See the Resources section on page 190 for some wonderful sources for organic, hard-to-find vegetables.) To keep their shape and color, I cook the pearl onions by themselves and add them to the *stifatho* just before serving.

Stewed Rabbit with Pearl Onions +
KOUNELI STIFATHO

I rabbit (3–4 pounds), cut into 8 serving pieces

I tablespoon kosher salt

I teaspoon freshly ground black pepper

4 tablespoons extra-virgin olive oil, plus more as needed

2 cups finely chopped yellow onions

$^1/_2$ cup dry red wine

$^1/_2$ cup red wine vinegar

$^1/_2$ cup water

I large ripe tomato, roughly chopped

2 bay leaves

I teaspoon finely chopped fresh oregano

I teaspoon finely chopped fresh thyme

I cinnamon stick

$^1/_4$ teaspoon freshly grated nutmeg

I pound red pearl onions

$^1/_3$ cup chopped fresh Italian (flat-leaf) parsley

Pat the rabbit pieces dry with paper towels and rub on all sides with the salt and pepper. Heat 2 tablespoons of the olive oil in a 12-inch nonaluminum skillet with sides about 3 inches high over high heat. This will allow you to brown all the rabbit pieces at once. If you don't have a skillet large enough, brown the rabbit in 2 batches, using I tablespoon of olive oil for each batch. Don't crowd the pieces in the pan or the rabbit will steam rather than brown.

Add the rabbit to the skillet and brown for about 4 minutes on each side. The meat tends to stick to the bottom of the pan, so monitor the pieces, turning gently with a metal spatula. When the pieces are golden brown on all sides, remove from the pan and set aside.

Reduce the heat to medium. If the pan is dry, add a little olive oil. Add the yellow onions and cook, stirring constantly, until the onions are a rich golden brown, about 5 minutes. Remove from the heat and add the wine, vinegar, and water. Return to medium heat and scrape the bottom of the pan with a spatula or spoon to deglaze, loosening any browned bits.

Add the tomato, bay leaves, oregano, thyme, cinnamon stick, and nutmeg to the liquid.

continued

Return the rabbit pieces to the pan and gently push the meat into the liquid. Reduce the heat to low, cover the skillet, and simmer until the rabbit is tender, 45 minutes to 1 hour.

While the rabbit is cooking, bring a saucepan half full of salted water to a boil. Add the pearl onions and cook for about 1 minute. Drain the onions and spread on a baking sheet to cool quickly. Cut off the root ends of the onions and slip off the skins.

In a skillet large enough to hold the pearl onions in a single layer, heat the remaining 2 tablespoons olive oil over medium-high heat. Add the onions and brown them evenly on all sides. Set aside.

Once the rabbit is tender, add the pearl onions to the stew and cook together for 3 to 5 minutes. Taste the sauce and adjust the seasoning.

Transfer the rabbit to a serving platter and spoon the sauce over the top. Garnish with the chopped parsley and serve.

SERVES 4

I decided early on that polenta was an extra-fancy version of grits, a staple of my childhood in Jackson, Mississippi. For me, polenta is a warm, cozy accompaniment to stew, roasted meats, and chicken, and a natural with any dish that has a sauce. There aren't many meals more warm and nurturing than *stifatho* and polenta. Two kinds of cheese make this polenta even more satisfying. Don't feel you have to stick with the cheeses suggested here. Try other cheeses, especially Greek cheeses such as Myzithra or ketalotyri, to see which flavors you prefer.

This is really two recipes in one. You can spoon this into bowls while it's soft and warm or make it the day before, refrigerate it in a dish overnight, and slice it for grilling the next day, a great option during warm weather.

A medium-grind cornmeal is fine for this polenta dish; if you can find it, fine-grind polenta is even better.

Polenta with Fontina and Parmesan

½ cup medium-grind polenta

½ cup semolina flour

2 cups Roasted Chicken Stock (page 184)

2 cups heavy cream

⅛ teaspoon freshly grated nutmeg

½ teaspoon kosher salt

¼ cup grated fontina cheese

¼ cup grated Parmesan cheese

Note: The parchment paper isn't absolutely necessary, but makes removing polenta from the pan extra easy!

In a small bowl, combine the polenta and semolina and set aside. Combine the stock, cream, nutmeg, and salt into a heavy saucepan and place over medium heat. Bring to a simmer and slowly but steadily whisk in the polenta mixture. Return to a simmer, stirring constantly, then reduce the heat so the mixture barely bubbles. Stir the polenta for about 5 more minutes, until it thickens and begins to pull away from the sides of the pan. Remove the pan from the heat. Sprinkle the grated cheeses over the hot polenta and mix well. If you like, serve it while it's soft and warm.

If you're making this dish the day before serving, spread the polenta while it's still warm in an ungreased round or 8-by-8-inch baking dish lined with parchment paper (see note). Let cool for about 10 minutes, then cover with plastic wrap. Refrigerate for at least 3 hours or overnight.

After the polenta has thoroughly chilled, loosen the edges by running a knife or spatula around the sides of the pan. Cut into wedges or 2-inch squares. Lift the pieces out carefully with a small spatula and place on a baking sheet. Grill or broil until golden brown. Serve immediately.

SERVES **6** TO **8**

Greeks serve many kinds of greens and always (or at least always in my family) give their greens a generous squeeze of fresh lemon juice. This recipe calls for a double hit of lemon—the juice from two large lemons as well as finely chopped preserved lemon. Once you have preserved lemons on hand, this recipe is quick and easy—and addictive, for those of us who love lemon.

The trick to using fresh spinach is washing the leaves carefully. I fill my sink with water, immerse the bunches, and play some good music while I make sure that each leaf is completely free of dirt and grit. Roll up the cleaned spinach in a paper towel to dry and refrigerate to crisp the leaves until you're ready to cook them.

Fresh Spinach with Preserved Lemons ◆
SPANAKI ME LEMONE

2 pounds fresh spinach, tough stems removed

$1/4$ cup extra-virgin olive oil, plus 2 tablespoons

6 cloves garlic, minced

Kosher salt and freshly cracked black pepper to taste

1 tablespoon finely chopped Preserved Lemon (page 188)

$1/4$ cup plus 2 tablespoons fresh lemon juice

Bring a large saucepan three-fourths full of salted water to a boil. Add the spinach, cover, and cook just until tender, 4 to 5 minutes. Take care not to overcook it. Place a colander in the sink and drain the spinach immediately. Let cool for 10 minutes.

In a large sauté pan, heat the $1/4$ cup olive oil over high heat. Add the garlic. Reduce the heat to medium-high, and cook until just barely browned, 1 to 2 minutes. Add the spinach and salt and pepper, and toss quickly. Add the preserved lemon and toss again. Remove from the heat, transfer to a plate, and drizzle with the 2 tablespoons olive oil and the lemon juice. Finish with more cracked pepper to taste.

SERVES **4** TO **6**

I can't taste these cookies without thinking about my godmother, Maria Costas. A true lady, Maria is the most glamorous woman I've ever met, always dressed to the nines, always the epitome of graciousness. Maria is a musician, a music teacher, and a fabulous singer as well as a terrific cook, and nobody makes *melomakarona* to rival hers.

Serve these dark, cakelike spice cookies beside fresh Black Mission figs, and they don't seem like cookies at all, which is appropriate given their history. *Melomakarona*, which literally translates to "honey buns," have been made in Greece for centuries. Whenever I eat them, I imagine platters of these cookies carried into a forum in ancient Greece alongside tall goblets of sweet wine, which is how they were originally served.

Made with orange zest, cinnamon, and nutmeg, these cookies have a sophisticated flavor, perfect with fresh figs and coffee or dessert wine at the end of a meal. A dunk in a cool honey syrup after the cookies come out of the oven brings out all the spices and adds a layer of sweetness. The allspice is a nod to the Greek tradition of adding sweet spices such as cinnamon to savory dishes (as in *kota kapama* on page 16) and adding spices that we consider to be savory to sweet treats.

Honey-Dipped Cookies with Fresh Figs •
MELOMAKARONA KAI SIKA

1 cup unsalted butter, at room temperature, plus extra for greasing

1 cup vegetable oil

1 cup sugar

2 eggs

1 cup whole milk

1/2 cup fresh orange juice

1/2 teaspoon baking soda

1 tablespoon baking powder

1/2 teaspoon ground cinnamon

1/2 teaspoon freshly grated nutmeg

1/2 teaspoon ground allspice (optional)

1/2 teaspoon salt

4 cups semolina flour

3 1/2 cups all-purpose flour

Syrup

6 cups sugar

2 cups honey

3 1/2 cups water

1 large lemon, juiced and then sliced

2 cups almonds or pecans, toasted (see note, page 30) and finely ground

In the bowl of a stand mixer fitted with the paddle attachment, beat the butter until light in color and fluffy, 12 to 15 minutes. Slowly add the oil in a steady stream until the butter and oil are incorporated. Add the sugar and beat until combined. Add the eggs, one at a time, beating well after each addition. Slowly add the milk as you did the oil, mixing constantly. The mixture should be very thick, like a mayonnaise.

In a small bowl, combine the orange juice and baking soda. Mix gently and add the foaming liquid to the butter mixture. Mix well until incorporated.

In another bowl, combine the baking powder, cinnamon, nutmeg, allspice, salt, and 1 cup of the semolina flour. Stir into the butter mixture just until the flour is moist. Add the remaining 3 cups semolina and the all-purpose flour in 5 batches, mixing after each addition. Mix until the dough binds together and can be handled easily. Cover and refrigerate until firm and thoroughly chilled, at least 2 hours.

While the dough chills, make the honey syrup. In a large heavy saucepan, combine the sugar, honey, water, lemon juice, and lemon slices. Simmer for 15 to 20 minutes, stirring to dissolve the sugar, then remove from the heat and let cool.

Preheat the oven to 350°F. Grease a baking sheet with butter.

Scoop up tablespoons of the dough, roll into balls, and place on the prepared baking sheet. Flatten into ovals about $1/8$ inch thick and arrange about 1 inch apart. Bake until lightly browned, 5 to 6 minutes. Transfer to a wire rack to cool. Repeat with the remaining dough.

Spread the ground nuts in an even layer on a plate. Set a wire rack over a baking sheet or parchment paper.

When the cookies are cooled, using tongs, dip each cookie in the honey syrup, then roll in the ground nuts. Let dry on the wire rack for 30 minutes before storing in an airtight container or lined cookie tins.

MAKES **3** DOZEN COOKIES

MENU

77 • Shrimp and Caper Salad
(GARITHOSALATA ME KAPPARI)

78 • Aegean Meatballs with Pita Bread
(KEFTETHAKIA KAI PITA)

79 • Cabbage Leaves Filled with Lamb
and Rice (DOLMATHES ME ARNI KAI RIZI)

80 • Skopeletti Stuffed Tomatoes
(DOMATES YEMISTES)

81 • Rolled Baklava (BAKLAVA ORTHI)

STOPPING AT A TAVERNA AFTER WANDERING THROUGH TOWN · Sampling shrimp with capers, Aegean meatballs, and *baklava orthi*

I saved a day to explore Skopelos on my own, climbing the steep stone stairs and cobblestone alleys that wind through the town. The thick, heavy stone of the buildings and stairs are whitewashed, but doors and window frames glow with deep, vibrant colors.

As I walked past open windows, I could hear and smell onion and garlic sautéing in the pan. The people inside were cooking their dinners just a few feet from where I walked. This closeness seemed new and wonderful for someone who hails from the American suburbs, where doors stand well back from the street, often hidden behind hedges and fences.

Hungry from all the aromas, I headed for the nearest taverna, the Greek version of a café. When you boat into Skopelos, you see the tavernas first, lined up facing the port. Almost always looking out over the water, almost always family run, the tavernas stay open from morning until late at night. You'll find people in the tavernas any time of the day, for an afternoon coffee, for a little bite to eat with a glass of ouzo, or for a meal when all the restaurants in town have closed. The best thing about the tavernas is that most people don't look at a menu; you just walk right into the kitchen to see what's cooking and you

point to what looks and smells most appealing. I chose a cold salad of bright pink shrimp with big, juicy capers, some gorgeous stuffed tomatoes, stuffed cabbage— a staple from my childhood—and, of course, baklava.

In the United States, comfort foods tend to be mild, like macaroni and cheese or chocolate pudding. In Greece, comfort foods are big-flavored and hearty (after all, they have to stand up to the taste of retsina, ouzo, and tsipouro, the three alcoholic beverages most popular in the tavernas of Skopelos). The savory flavors are what I like best about Greece tavernas. Every dish on this menu is comfort food, through and through, and every dish is filled with flavor. Unless you open your own taverna, you probably won't make all of these dishes at the same time, but any one or two of them makes a satisfying lunch or a cozy dinner.

Most people think of capers, or *kappari*, as exclusively Italian, but I've always thought their flavor was perfect in Greek foods. The briny, piquant flavor makes me think of a sun-drenched hillside next to blue water, which for me means Skopelos. The Greeks have cooked with capers for millennia; historians note that Greeks brought capers to Gaul as early as 600 B.C.

These days, if you stop in a Greek taverna, you'll often find large capers set out in small bowls as *mezes*, appetizers. Try these with a sip of ouzo—flavors don't get more intense than this.

In my kitchen I really like a final sprinkling of capers over roasted vegetables, especially red peppers, eggplant, and Brussels sprouts (see page 19), and I'm a big fan of piccata sauce made with capers, lemon, fresh parsley, and butter. But I like capers best with seafood—both have the flavor of sun and sea—and I think combining shrimp and capers makes each one taste better.

One clove of garlic gives the shrimp a subtle flavor. If you like a heartier flavor, double the garlic in this recipe.

I serve this as a first course, as a quick, light dinner, or as a leisurely weekend brunch. Add cherry tomatoes when they're in season. Serve on a bed of young field greens if you like.

2 pounds medium shrimp, peeled, deveined, and tails cut off

1 clove garlic, minced

3 tablespoons fresh lemon juice

1 teaspoon red pepper flakes

2 scallions, white and tender green parts, finely chopped

1 cup finely chopped red onion

2 tablespoons capers, drained

1 celery stalk, finely chopped

30 cherry tomatoes, halved (optional)

Dressing

2 teaspoons finely chopped fresh oregano

3 tablespoons extra-virgin olive oil

1/2 teaspoon kosher salt

Freshly ground black pepper to taste

1 tablespoon fresh lemon juice

1 tablespoon red wine vinegar

2 teaspoons finely chopped fresh Italian (flat-leaf) parsley

Shrimp and Caper Salad •
GARITHOSALATA ME KAPPARI

Bring a large saucepan three-fourths full of salted water to a boil over high heat. Add the shrimp and simmer until pink, about 5 minutes. Drain the shrimp and rinse quickly under cold water.

Meanwhile, in a bowl, combine the garlic, lemon juice, and red pepper flakes. Add the hot shrimp to the garlic mixture and marinate for 10 minutes.

In a large bowl, toss together the shrimp with the marinade, the scallions, red onion, capers, celery, and tomatoes.

To make the dressing, in a small bowl, whisk together the oregano, olive oil, salt, pepper, lemon juice, and vinegar. Pour over the shrimp and vegetables, add the parsley, and toss to incorporate. Cover and refrigerate until ready to eat. Serve chilled.

SERVES **4** TO **6**

These savory little meatballs are the perfect dress-them-up, dress-them-down food. Stuff these meatballs into pita, spoon on some Cucumber Yogurt (page 58), and you've got a good-for-you portable meal just right while ferrying the kids to Little League or a soccer game. Or arrange them on a beautiful platter beside a pretty bowl of the Cucumber Yogurt and they're an ideal appetizer before a formal dinner.

On Skopelos, I got the chance to make them with oregano I had just gathered on the hillsides. If you make these with just-picked oregano, your meatballs are a guaranteed hit.

These meatballs freeze well. Cook extras, pop them into a lock-top plastic bag, seal tightly, and freeze so you always have a few batches on hand for a quick, wholesome supper.

Aegean Meatballs with Pita Bread ◆
KEFTETHAKIA KAI PITA

I pound lean ground beef

$^1/_2$ cup whole milk

I $^1/_2$ slices white bread with crust

$^1/_2$ cup chopped yellow onion

I clove garlic, minced

I tablespoon finely chopped fresh mint

$^1/_4$ cup finely chopped fresh oregano or other fresh herbs

I teaspoon kosher salt

$^1/_2$ teaspoon freshly ground black pepper

I large egg

$^1/_4$ cup extra-virgin olive oil

I teaspoon white wine vinegar or distilled white vinegar

Flour for dusting

$^1/_4$ cup vegetable or light olive oil

6 rounds of pita bread, cut in quarters

Preheat the oven to 400°F. Line a 9-by-13-inch baking dish with aluminum foil.

Place the ground beef in a large bowl. In another bowl, pour the milk over the bread, soak for 2 minutes, then squeeze out the excess milk. Crumble up the bread and add to the bowl with the meat. Add the onion, garlic, mint, oregano, salt, and pepper and mix well. Add the egg, olive oil, and vinegar and mix again.

Roll the mixture into walnut-sized portions and dust with flour. Once all the meatballs are formed, heat the vegetable oil in a large sauté pan over high heat until hot but not smoking. Reduce the heat to medium and add the meatballs. Brown on all sides, 2 to 3 minutes, and drain on paper towels. Transfer to the prepared dish and bake until cooked through, about 15 minutes.

Serve with several quarters of the pita bread on each plate, then stuff the pita with meatballs and top with Cucumber Yogurt (page 58).

SERVES 4 TO 6

Greeks are very big on stuffing vegetables, and I'm always amazed at how many different fillings they create. This filling of lamb and rice is hearty and soul-satisfying. Compare this dish—a twist on *dolmathes*, with cabbage taking the place of grape leaves—with the stuffed tomatoes that follow. Both follow the same idea, but the results couldn't be more different. If you want to try your own "Stuffed Vegetable Fest," pair these stuffed cabbage leaves with the Bell Peppers Stuffed with Meat and Rice on page 46. If you have trouble finding Myzithra cheese, see the Resources section on page 190.

Cabbage Leaves Filled with Lamb and Rice • DOLMATHES ME ARNI KAI RIZI

I large cabbage, cored

$^3/_4$ cup extra-virgin olive oil

I cup finely chopped yellow onion

I pound lean ground lamb or beef

$^3/_4$ cup uncooked regular-grain white rice

2 cloves garlic, finely chopped

Pinch of red pepper flakes

I teaspoon chopped fresh oregano

3 scallions, white and tender green parts, finely chopped

I cup finely chopped fresh Italian (flat-leaf) parsley

I teaspoon kosher salt

$^1/_2$ teaspoon freshly ground black pepper

I$^1/_2$ cups Roasted Chicken Stock (page 184) or beef broth

Juice of I lemon

Sauce

Juice of 2 lemons

3 eggs

I cup hot Roasted Chicken Stock (page 184) or beef broth

I cup grated Myzithra cheese

Note: Tempering means to add a few spoonfuls of the hot liquid into the egg mixture while whisking vigorously. Add the remaining hot liquid slowly, whisking constantly to keep the eggs from hardening or scrambling.

Bring a stockpot three-fourths full of salted water to a boil. Carefully separate the leaves of the cabbage and submerge them in the pot. Blanch briefly, 3 to 4 minutes. Drain and set aside.

Heat $^1/_4$ cup of the olive oil in a large skillet over medium-high heat and add the onion. Cook until soft, about 3 minutes. Add the lamb and brown lightly. Add the rice and stir until each grain is coated with the juices and oil. Reduce the heat to medium-low and add the garlic, red pepper flakes, oregano, scallions, parsley, salt, pepper, and $^1/_2$ cup of the stock. Cover and simmer until the rice is tender, about 20 minutes. Add a little water if the pan is dry. Remove from the heat and let the filling cool slightly.

Pour the remaining $^1/_2$ cup olive oil into a large, clean pot over low heat. Place I tablespoon of filling in the center of a cabbage leaf, near the stem end. Fold over each side and roll upward, as if you're forming a burrito. Taking care not to burn yourself, place the filled leaf in the pot, seam side down. Continue filling and rolling leaves until you've used all the filling. Pour the remaining I cup stock into the pot and add the lemon juice. Place a plate on top of the cabbage packets to keep them submerged. Cover, bring to a boil over high heat, reduce the heat to low, and simmer until the cabbage leaves are tender, about 2 hours. Add water if necessary. Remove from the heat.

Meanwhile, make the sauce: In a bowl, whisk together the lemon juice and eggs. The trick to this sauce is to temper the egg mixture by first ladling in just a spoonful of the hot stock while you whisk (see note) to keep the eggs from hardening or scrambling. Slowly ladle in the remaining hot stock while continuing to whisk until all the stock has been added.

To serve, place the stuffed cabbage packets on a large platter, pour the sauce over the cabbage, and sprinkle with the cheese.

SERVES 4 TO 6

If you're a tomato fan, as I am, you'll like this method of cooking them. You scoop out the center of the tomato and combine the pulp with rice, fresh herbs, onion, and garlic. Add pine nuts and black currants and spoon this delicious mixture back into the tomato. When you bake these tomatoes, the topping of kasseri cheese becomes a rich, golden crust. If you can't find kasseri cheese, see Resources on page 190.

Skopeletti Stuffed Tomatoes •
DOMATES YEMISTES

6 ripe beefsteak tomatoes

$1/4$ cup extra-virgin olive oil, plus 4 teaspoons

2 cups diced yellow onions

I large clove garlic, minced

6 tablespoons uncooked long-grain white rice

2 tablespoons finely chopped fresh Italian (flat-leaf) parsley

$1/4$ cup pine nuts, toasted (see note, page 30)

$1/4$ cup black currants (optional)

I tablespoon finely chopped fresh dill

$1/4$ teaspoon kosher salt

$1/8$ teaspoon freshly ground black pepper

$1/2$ cup grated kasseri cheese

Slice the tops off of the tomatoes and scoop out the pulp, leaving shells approximately $1/2$ inch thick. Reserve the pulp.

Preheat the oven to 375°F.

In a sauté pan, heat the $1/4$ cup olive oil over medium heat. Add the onions and cook until golden brown, about 5 minutes. Add the garlic, rice, and reserved tomato pulp and simmer for 5 minutes. Stir in the parsley, pine nuts, currants, dill, salt, and pepper.

Divide the filling among the tomato shells and place the stuffed tomatoes in a 9-by-13-inch baking dish. Sprinkle the tops with the cheese and drizzle with the 4 teaspoons olive oil. Pour I cup of water into the bottom of the dish and bake until the cheese forms a golden brown crust, about I hour.

SERVES 6

The hillside villages of the islands in the Aegean Sea are one of the only places you'll find this type of baklava made this way—rolled up in a coil rather than layered in a baking dish and cut into squares. This baklava takes less time to make and has its own unique flavor. Rolled baklava also makes an ideal finger food for parties when cut into small pieces and set out in fluted foil cups. This recipe makes enough to serve a party of twelve to twenty-five people; cut the recipe in half if you don't want to hand out a little bag of these treats to your guests as they leave. For a twist, drizzle chocolate over them after they cool.

See "Tips for Handling Phyllo Dough" on page 39 before you begin this recipe.

Rolled Baklava • BAKLAVA ORTHI

Syrup

2 1/4 cups sugar

1 1/2 cups water

1/4 cup honey

Two thin lemon slices

1 cinnamon stick

3 whole cloves

1 pound blanched almonds, coarsely ground

2 tablespoons sugar

1 pound walnuts, toasted (see note, page 30) and coarsely ground

2 1/2 cups (5 sticks) unsalted butter

1 1/2 teaspoons ground cinnamon

1/8 teaspoon ground cloves

1 1/2 pounds phyllo dough (32 sheets)

Combine all of the syrup ingredients in a heavy saucepan and bring to a boil. Reduce the heat to low and simmer for 15 minutes. Remove from the heat, remove the lemon slices and spices, and let cool to room temperature.

Preheat the oven to 375°F. Have ready an ungreased baking sheet. Place a wire rack over another baking sheet or parchment paper.

Place the almonds and 1 tablespoon of the sugar in a food processor fitted with the metal blade. Pulse until coarsely ground. (Adding the sugar coats the nuts and helps keep them from turning into a paste if overprocessed.) Transfer to a bowl and set aside. Place the walnuts and remaining 1 tablespoon sugar in the processor and pulse as you did the almonds.

In a saucepan, melt the butter slowly over very low heat.

Thoroughly combine the ground almonds and walnuts, cinnamon, and cloves in a bowl. On a clean, dry work surface, layer 4 sheets of phyllo dough, brushing each sheet with melted butter and gently pressing the sheets together as you go. Once the 4 sheets are pressed together, sprinkle 1 cup of the nut mixture evenly over the top sheet. Starting on a long side, carefully fold over the edge and roll the sheets into as tight a cylinder as possible without breaking the phyllo. Repeat with the remaining phyllo sheets, 4 at a time, and remaining nut mixture, to make 8 cylinders.

Cut each roll into 2-inch pieces. Dip each piece into the melted butter and place as many as will fit on the baking sheet. Bake until golden brown, 25 to 30 minutes. Remove from the oven and, using tongs, lift each piece from the pan, dip in the syrup, and place on the wire rack to drain. If the syrup begins to thicken, reheat it slightly over very low heat. Repeat baking and dipping with the remaining pieces of baklava.

Serve in small fluted paper serving cups or small cupcake liners arranged on a platter.

MAKES 72 PIECES

My Restaurant Kitchens in

NORTHERN CALIFORNIA

I came home from Greece excited about bringing new ideas into my restaurant kitchen. I'd always sought out organic, locally grown produce, but watching my aunt and uncle gather greens from the hills around their home or cook fish just minutes out of the ocean made me even more committed to simple, fresh foods in my restaurants. My style of cooking leans toward rustic foods with an elegant twist—for example, my Pan-Seared Halibut and Sweet Corn Zabaglione (page 113). I've always liked to mix country and uptown flavors, and I still do.

But I also wanted more authenticity in the foods I cooked. I worked to re-create the flavors I'd tasted and the aromas that had surrounded me in Greece. While taking the ferry from Skopelos, I'd watched as a group of Gypsies unwrapped their lunch. I took a deep breath, trying to memorize the unfamiliar but distinct fragrance that wafted over. After a long search, I found the source of that aroma—fennel growing wild along the roadside in Greece—and then I hunted again until I found a seasoning with the same distinct fragrance—wild fennel pollen. I have those Gypsies to thank for my signature dish of Spicy Gypsy Mussels (page 101).

You'll notice many seafood dishes in this section of the book. My visit to Greece made me rethink how I serve fish in my restaurants. While in Greece, I tasted so many different, amazing seafood dishes—most of them cooked in home kitchens—that when I returned to California, I came up with ways to lure my patrons to try the fish. When I first put a whole roasted fish on the menu at Bistro Don Giovanni, I went so far as to guarantee to take the fish back—and cook anything else on the menu to replace it—if the person who ordered the fish didn't absolutely love it. (Nobody ever took me up on that offer.)

And then there's my Seafood Fest, a tradition that began one summer when my parents were coming to town and one of my fish vendors showed me so much beautiful fresh seafood, I couldn't choose just two or three things. I practically bought out his entire stock and then created a whole menu to showcase the gorgeous prawns, lobsters, and clams.

This section of the book is a little more daring than the first two sections—but it's also a blast! If you try my recipe for Whole Fish Roasted with Fennel, Olives, and Chilies (page 87), you'll be surprised by how self-sufficient you'll feel cooking and serving a whole fish. Or a whole wood-fired lobster stuffed with crab (page 136). Or prawns in a grappa cream sauce (page 134).

Less experienced cooks should not be intimidated by any of these seafood dishes. Cooking the fish is the easy part. The trick is to find fresh, fresh seafood, and that's just a matter of seeking out a good fishmonger near you. Not sure where to find fresh seafood? Ask at a restaurant that serves great fish—or find somebody who's part Greek. All my Greek friends who live far from the sea still manage to locate good fresh fish.

MENU

87 • Whole Fish Roasted with Fennel, Olives, and Chilies (PSARI PSITO)

90 • Tomato Bread Soup (DOMATO SOUPA ME PSOMI)

92 • Pampered White Beans (FASSOLIA)

94 • Grilled Asparagus with Tangerine Aioli (SPARANGI TIS SKARAS ME MANTARINI SALTSA)

96 • Orange-Scented Almond Cookies (AMYGTHALOTA ME PORTAKALI)

ROASTING A WHOLE FISH · I cook for one of my inspirations, Jacques Pépin

In Greece, if I brought a fish to the table without its head and tail, my Greek family would think I had lost my mind. It would be like bringing a roasted duck or goose to the table without its skin. When I was the chef at Bistro Don Giovanni, we were one of the first restaurants in the Napa Valley to offer a whole roasted fish, and in the beginning we had to work to persuade people to try it. Within a few months, though, a whole roasted fish was one of our most popular dishes.

Robert Mondavi was a favorite customer because he loved having a whole fish brought to the table—one evening he brought in Jacques Pépin and ordered this dish. (My staff and I were absolutely thrilled to peek out into the dining room and see Jacques sitting at his table!) Soon afterward, Jacques wrote a letter to the James Beard Foundation on my behalf, and that led to my first James Beard dinner—and all because I refused to cut the head and tail off my fish!

This recipe connects me to so many restaurant kitchens and to so many chefs who taught and inspired me—Georges Blanc and Roger Vergé, whom I worked with in France, a dream come true for a young chef; Melissa Kelly at the Old Chatham Sheepherding Company Inn, where I worked for the first time as a sous chef; Larry Forgione at the Beekman 1766 Tavern. Each of these generous chefs served as an example of how to make a restaurant the best place in the world to work.

I'm sharing my roasted fish history to convince you to try it. Roasting a whole fish is easy—honestly, you'll be surprised at how simple it is. Don't be afraid of the head and the tail. Just as a chicken tastes best roasted whole, so does fish taste best cleaned and roasted in one piece with the bones and juices still inside. I believe fresh fish roasted whole has a flavor that's completely true to the sea.

Because a whole roasted fish feels rustic to me—in the best possible way—the rest of this menu is country fare, too, whole and hearty and completely satisfying. A tomato soup made with country bread and a fine grating of cheese perfectly suits the roasted fish. Hearty beans, tender and full of flavor, get a lift from rosemary and thyme, onion and carrots. Grilled asparagus with a sparkling fresh citrus aioli adds a bright note to the meal. I like to end with a very traditional sweet: delicate almond cookies flavored very subtly with orange flower water, a flavor brought to Greece by the Persians. For the best flavor and texture, make these cookies the Greek way—at least three days before you plan to serve them.

There are just three steps to roasting a fish whole, and none of them are hard. First, pan-sear your fish in a large sauté pan on top of the stove. Then take the fish out, add thin slices of fennel, and put the fish back in the pan; the fennel slices absorb the flavor of the broth, the fish, and the chilies. Finally, roast the fish in the oven. You can grill a whole fish if you prefer, but be sure to finish it in the oven so the juices of the fish have a chance to mingle with the herbs and spices.

I like to serve a whole fish to each person. This recipe explains how to cook four whole fish in a home kitchen. You'll have to sauté two fish at a time, but you can roast them all at once; use a large roasting pan and don't overlap the fish. If you're serving two people, just halve this recipe.

I like snapper (particularly red or Thai snapper), but you can use this cooking method with just about any fresh, firm-fleshed fish, such as striped bass, *rouge*, black bass, or trout. Try it with any whole fish that's between one and two pounds.

I love the flavor of Calabrian chilies with fish. You can find them packed in oil in specialty stores, or see Resources, page 190.

Whole Fish Roasted with Fennel, Olives, and Chilies • PSARI PSITO

4 whole snappers, about 1 1/2 pounds each, cleaned and gutted

1 tablespoon kosher salt

2 teaspoons freshly ground black pepper

1 cup extra-virgin olive oil

1 medium fennel bulb, thinly sliced

3 cups fish or vegetable stock

2 teaspoons chopped fresh thyme

4 teaspoons chopped Calabrian chilies (see Resources, page 190) or 2 teaspoons red pepper flakes

1/2 cup black olives, pitted and halved

1/2 cup chopped fresh Italian (flat-leaf) parsley

Preheat the oven to 450°F.

Rinse the fish in cool water and pat dry with paper towels. Rub each fish with 3/4 teaspoon salt and 1/2 teaspoon pepper. Heat 1/2 cup of the olive oil in a 12-inch sauté pan over medium-high heat. Add two of the fish to the pan and sear on each side until golden brown, 3 to 4 minutes per side.

Remove the fish from the pan and pour off the excess oil. Place half of the fennel slices in the pan and lay the seared fish on top of the fennel. Add 1 1/2 cups of the stock, bring to a simmer over medium-high heat, and immediately remove from the heat. Carefully transfer the fish and fennel slices to a large roasting pan, cover, and set aside. Discard the cooking liquid. Repeat with the remaining fish, 1/2 cup olive oil, fennel slices, and stock.

Roast, covered, until the fish is cooked through, 20 to 25 minutes. Warm 4 plates during the last few minutes of cooking. Remove the pan from the oven, carefully set the fish aside, and divide the fennel into four servings. Spoon a serving onto each of the warmed plates and place a whole fish on top of the fennel. Transfer the liquid from the roasting pan to a saucepan. Add the thyme, chilies, and olives and bring to a simmer. Pour over the fish and garnish with the parsley.

SERVES 4

Buying Fresh Fish

If cooking fish is new to you, seek out a good source for fresh seafood. Check farmers' markets or ask your favorite restaurant where they buy their fish. When buying a whole fish, be sure to pick it up and smell it. A fresh fish feels firm in your hands and smells more of the sea than "fishy." Scales should be smooth and shiny and the eyes should be clear. Look at the gills to be sure they're bright pink or red, not gray or brown. Whenever possible, have your fishmonger clean the fish—most will be happy to do this for you.

This is a true country soup, and my Aunt Demetra would approve of its hearty, rustic, slowly simmered flavors. This tastes best with tomatoes picked and canned from your own garden, but, lacking those, I like to use San Marzano canned tomatoes. Experiment with the best tomatoes you have available, and see how this soup changes subtly depending on whether you use a fresh Early Girl or a plum (Roma) tomato.

I love adding the rind from Parmigiano-Reggiano to soups. The last bits of cheese fall from the rind, adding a flavor that everyone can taste but few can identify. Don't worry if the tiny chunks of Parmesan don't melt completely—that's the beauty of it. Pull the rind out of the soup just before you ladle it into bowls. See Resources on page 190 for some great cheeses.

Tomato Bread Soup •
DOMATO SOUPA ME PSOMI

½ cup extra-virgin olive oil

2 cups diced yellow onions

3 tablespoons coarsely chopped fresh basil

I large clove garlic, minced

One 28-ounce can crushed tomatoes

3 cups water

I cup Roasted Chicken Stock (page 184)

Two cups 2-inch bread cubes cut from a rustic loaf with the crust left on

I tablespoon kosher salt

¾ teaspoon freshly ground black pepper

About 3 inches of Parmigiano-Reggiano cheese rind (optional)

4 tablespoons freshly grated Parmesan or kasseri cheese for garnish (optional)

Heat the olive oil over medium heat in a large saucepan. Add the onions and cook until soft and clear. Add the basil and garlic and sauté for 2 to 3 minutes. Add the tomatoes, water, and stock and heat just to a boil. Reduce the heat to medium-low and simmer for 30 minutes.

Add the bread cubes, salt, pepper, and the cheese rind, if using, and simmer for 10 minutes longer.

Taste and adjust the seasoning. Serve hot, garnished with the grated cheese, if using.

SERVES 4 TO 6

Most people treat beans like soup, turning up the heat and walking away. I treat beans more like risotto, staying close by and stirring them often so every bean cooks evenly. Garlic, fresh rosemary and thyme, onion, and olive oil infuse my white beans with flavor—to me, these beans taste the way a sunny day in the Aegean feels. You can make your beans more tender by stirring every ten minutes. I like to add the salt three-quarters of the way through cooking so the beans absorb just the right amount. For a little heat, add a pinch of chili flakes.

If possible, soak your dried beans overnight and pour off the water before cooking. This is one of those soups that tastes even better a few days later, so it's a great meal to make on the weekend and serve during the week.

Pampered White Beans • FASSOLIA

I pound dried white beans

$^1/_2$ cup extra-virgin olive oil

I cup diced yellow onions

$^1/_2$ cup finely diced celery

$^1/_2$ cup finely diced carrot

2 teaspoons finely chopped fresh rosemary

9 cups water

3 $^1/_2$ teaspoons kosher salt

I teaspoon freshly ground black pepper

I teaspoon finely chopped fresh thyme or fresh oregano

In a bowl, cover the beans with cold water and soak overnight. Drain just before cooking.

Heat $^1/_4$ cup of the olive oil in a saucepan over medium-high heat. Add the onion, celery, and carrot, and sauté until the onion is soft and clear, 10 to 12 minutes. Add the rosemary, drained soaked beans, and water, and bring to a boil. Reduce the heat to medium and simmer, uncovered, for I hour, stirring every 10 minutes. Add I $^1/_2$ teaspoons of the salt and continue to simmer until the beans are tender, about 30 minutes longer. Stir in the remaining 2 teaspoons salt and $^1/_4$ cup olive oil, the pepper, and the thyme. Serve immediately.

SERVES 4

When asparagus is in season, I cook this dish every week. You can dress it up for a frou-frou formal dinner, but it's easy enough to set out with a simple salad or burgers. I made this aioli after seeing stall after stall of beautiful citrus fruit in the farmers' market in Athens. You can substitute just about any citrus juice for the tangerine in this recipe: try it with Meyer lemons or the juice from really beautiful oranges.

Grilled Asparagus with Tangerine Aioli •
SPARANGI TIS SKARAS ME MANTARINI SALTSA

Tangerine Aioli

2 cups fresh tangerine juice

2 egg yolks

I small clove garlic, minced

2 teaspoons fresh lemon juice

2 ¼ cups extra-virgin olive oil

I teaspoon kosher salt

½ teaspoon freshly ground black pepper

Asparagus

1 ½ pounds large asparagus stalks

Extra-virgin olive oil for brushing

¾ teaspoon kosher salt

½ teaspoon freshly ground black pepper

To make the aioli, in a saucepan, bring the tangerine juice to a boil over medium-high heat. Reduce the heat to a simmer and cook until reduced to a little more than I cup, about 8 minutes. Remove from the heat and let cool.

Combine the egg yolks, garlic, and lemon juice in a blender or food processor. Process at medium-high speed to blend, then very slowly add the 2 ¼ cups olive oil in a thin stream through the pouring hole while the machine is running. When the mixture has thickened, turn off the machine, add the reduced tangerine juice, and pulse until well mixed. Add the salt and pepper. If the aioli is too thick, add a little water. Refrigerate while you prepare the asparagus.

Prepare a fire in a charcoal grill or preheat a gas grill to high.

Bring a saucepan three-fourths full of salted water to a boil. Snap off the tough end of each asparagus spear and with a vegetable peeler or paring knife peel halfway up the stalk. Add the asparagus to the boiling water and blanch for 3 to 4 minutes. While the asparagus is cooking, pour ice water into a large bowl. Drain the asparagus and immediately immerse in the ice water to stop the cooking. Drain again.

Brush the asparagus with olive oil and season with the salt and pepper. Grill until tender-crisp, about 2 minutes on each side. Let cool. To serve, top with the aioli.

SERVES **4**

My grandmother Nina Cora made these delicate little no-bake cookies for special occasions. She flavored them with rose water, which is traditional and very, very subtle. I find orange flower water gives these a little extra zing. Look in specialty stores for orange flower water, or see Resources on page 190.

As with so many Greek treats, these are definitely make-ahead cookies. They're too delicate to eat the day they're made, but take on just the right consistency and flavor after you've let them stand for three days.

Orange-Scented Almond Cookies •
AMYGTHALOTA ME PORTAKALI

In a blender or a food processor, grind the almonds with $2 \frac{1}{2}$ cups of the confectioners' sugar until the mixture is the consistency of a fine, dry meal.

In a small saucepan over medium-high heat, bring the orange juice and orange flower water to a simmer. Remove from the heat and immediately add the almond mixture, stirring well until the ingredients are thoroughly combined into a moist paste. Let cool.

Form tablespoons of the batter into the shape of small pears, each approximately 1 inch high. (Dip your fingers into a little orange juice to help you shape the cookies more easily.) Place the remaining $\frac{1}{2}$ cup of confectioners' sugar on a plate and dredge each cookie thoroughly. Wrap each cookie individually in cellophane or place in a box with a tight lid. Let stand at room temperature for at least 3 days before serving.

3 cups blanched almonds

3 cups confectioners' sugar

$\frac{1}{4}$ cup fresh orange juice, plus a little extra to shape the cookies

1 tablespoon orange flower water

MAKES **25** TO **30** COOKIES

MENU

101 • Spicy Gypsy Mussels (MYTHIAS)

102 • Rustic Kalamata Olive Bread
(ELIOPITA)

104 • Grilled Grape Leaves Filled with Goat Cheese
(DOLMATHESTIS SKARA ME TIRI)

106 • Harvest Chicken with *Vinocotto*
(KOTO ME VINOCOTTO)

107 • Stawberry-Topped
Vanilla Custards (CREMOSAS)

MAKING A HARVEST CHICKEN WITH FRESH GRAPES AND *VINOCOTTO* • This meal reminds me of the Gypsies in Greece and the grape crush in California's wine country

A hydrofoil zips you across the Aegean Sea from Skopelos to Athens in about two hours. The ferry, slower and more colorful, makes the same trip in four to six hours, stopping for people at dozens of ports along the way.

I sat outside on the ferry watching as a group of Gypsies boarded at Corfu. The little girls wore faded, once-bright skirts and rough sandals, and the women had thick scarves covering their heads. At lunch time, while the rest of the passengers bought packaged sandwiches from the snack bar, the Gypsies opened paper bags and pulled out foil packets. I didn't want to appear too curious so I kept my seat—but I tried to figure out what they were eating from the delicious smells that wafted over to me. I could identify stuffed grape leaves, wild onions and garlic, fish and tomatoes; there was also an intense fennel scent that I couldn't quite place.

When I returned to my own kitchen in California, I created my signature dish at Postino, a spicy bowl of mussels, inspired by the aromas of the Gypsy meal onboard the ferry. The secret ingredient in this dish is wild fennel pollen, which can be ordered from specialty-foods stores (see Resources on page 190). I love the flavor of this spice. It's so concentrated, it's almost an extract—like getting a case or two of fennel in one tiny little jar. I also add Calabrian chilies to my mussels because they have some heat but they're not on fire in your mouth.

Serve a rustic, country-style bread with the mussels so you can dip into the broth. Try my easy recipe for *eliopita*, a Greek olive bread with lots of Kalamata olives. Brushing on milk during the last ten minutes of cooking gives the bread a nice gloss. If you don't have time to make *eliopita*, any crusty bread will work.

Grape leaves filled with goat cheese are just the right complement to the Gypsy mussels—smooth, cool, rich, and tangy—just what you want after the spiciness of the mussels.

I created the harvest chicken dish on this menu one autumn during the grape crush while in the Napa Valley. Just-picked wine grapes move up and down the valley in big gondolas during grape crush, and they taste and smell so wonderful, I just had to cook with them. The sauce for this chicken gives you two layers of flavor, both pulled from the fruit of the vine: the first is the light, fruity taste of fresh grapes heated with the chicken until just warmed through. The second layer of flavor runs deeper; it comes from *vinocotto*, an earthy, sweet and tangy reduction of grape must, popular in Italy since ancient times.

For me, the mark of a great meal is one that takes into account the textures of each dish. Set out spicy mussels, tangy grape leaves filled with smooth, creamy goat cheese, and the fresh, fruity yet complex harvest chicken, and you'll see what I mean.

The dessert with this meal has to be light, and an airy *cremosa* is as light as you can get. I change this recipe from season to season, adding fresh berries in summer and fresh Black Mission figs or a dried fruit conserve in the fall.

Watching the Gypsies on the ferry at Corfu made me think about cooking with ingredients from the wild—mussels taken right from the shore, wild onions growing by the side of the road. Most of us can't gather our own ingredients, but I think wild fennel pollen (see Resources, page 190) is a way to add a Gypsy flavor to many fish and chicken dishes.

There isn't really a substitute for wild fennel pollen. Like saffron, wild fennel pollen is expensive by volume, but a half pinch adds incredible flavor. To make the most of wild fennel pollen, don't stir it into the sauce but sprinkle it over the mussels just before serving.

This dish also calls for ouzo, which is the most popular drink in Greece. Look for ouzo in a good wine store. Place the bottle on the table when you serve the mussels, and either drink it over ice or neat with a side of water.

If you have all the ingredients ready to go, these mussels cook very quickly, and they make a spectacular—yet very easy—appetizer for four to six people. You can double or even triple the recipe to make a main course. Serve with a salad of field greens and crusty bread for dunking into the broth.

Spicy Gypsy Mussels • MYTHIAS

2 pounds mussels, preferably Prince Edward Island

$1/3$ cup extra-virgin olive oil

3 cloves garlic, thinly sliced

1 tablespoon chopped Calabrian chilies (see Resources, page 190) or red pepper flakes

2 tablespoons ouzo

1 cup dry white wine

One 14 $1/2$-ounce can pureed tomatoes

1 teaspoon coarsely chopped fresh oregano

1 tablespoon unsalted butter

Kosher salt and freshly ground black pepper to taste

Wild fennel pollen for garnish

Scrub the mussels under cold water and pull off any beards.

Over medium-high heat, warm the olive oil in a large sauté pan and add the garlic. Toast the garlic until golden brown, 1 to 2 minutes. Stir in the chilies, heat for 1 minute, then add the mussels and ouzo to the pan. Toss quickly and let the liquid reduce for 1 minute.

Add the wine and cook for 2 to 3 minutes. Add the tomatoes and oregano, reduce the heat to low, and simmer for about 5 minutes. Swirl in the butter, season with salt and pepper, and sprinkle on a pinch of wild fennel pollen just before serving.

SERVES **4** TO **6**

I've never had an olive bread filled with more olives than this one. *Eliopita* isn't a yeast bread, so it's quick and easy; you mix all the ingredients in one step before kneading. If there's any bread left over the next day, slice and toast it for great bruschetta or crostini. It's also wonderful served with *taramosalata* (page 34). Two tips when baking this bread: Brush the top with milk during the last ten minutes of cooking, and be sure to use good olives.

Rustic Kalamata Olive Bread • ELIOPITA

In a sauté pan, heat 2 tablespoons of the olive oil over medium heat and add the onion. Cook until lightly browned but not fully caramelized, 2 to 3 minutes. Set aside to cool.

In a large bowl, combine the flour, baking powder, and salt. Add the cooled onion to the dry ingredients. Add the warm water, the remaining 4 tablespoons olive oil, the thyme, and the olives. Mix until the dough comes together in a rough mass. Turn out onto a floured board and knead until the dough is soft and smooth, 5 to 8 minutes. Cover with a kitchen towel and let rise for about 20 minutes.

Preheat the oven to 400°F.

Shape the dough into a large ball and place in a greased loaf pan. Bake for 50 minutes. Brush the top of the loaf with milk and bake for another 10 minutes, or until the bread is golden brown with a nice sheen. Remove from the oven and let cool.

SERVES **4** TO **6**

6 tablespoons extra-virgin olive oil

1 medium yellow onion, finely chopped

4 cups sifted all-purpose flour

1 tablespoon baking powder

1 teaspoon kosher salt

$^3/_4$ cup warm water

1 tablespoon finely chopped fresh thyme

1 cup pitted and chopped Kalamata olives

Milk for brushing

Dolmathes appear in many different forms—stuffed with meat, stuffed with a mixture of rice and lamb, cold, warm, grilled, and even cloaked in a luscious egg and lemon sauce. Combining my Greek roots with my California style of cooking, this recipe fills grape leaves with a cool, tangy goat cheese. Try these *dolmathes* on a picnic, for brunch, as an afternoon pick-me-up, or as an appetizer for dinner.

In every market in Greece, you find grapevine leaves for *dolmathes*—big, perfect leaves that look like they were picked a few minutes earlier. Once you've visited Skopelos, you realize nobody who lives there buys vine leaves from the market— they step outside their door to the nearest vine.

When I was eight, my mom built a trellis and planted grapevines at our home in Jackson, Mississippi. Now her vine leaves grow to be as big as dinner plates, and they're just as beautiful as any I saw in Greece. Like those cooks in Greece, my mom picks her leaves, blanches them lightly, covers them with oil, salt, and pepper, and they're ready for *dolmathes*.

Those of us who don't have grapevines right outside our door have to turn to grape leaves brined in jars, which work just fine. I tend to buy bottled grape leaves imported from Greece (see Resources on page 190), but I think American leaves work well, too.

8 ounces goat cheese

I tablespoon chopped mixed fresh herbs such as thyme, basil, rosemary, and parsley

$1/_2$ teaspoon kosher salt

$1/_8$ teaspoon freshly ground black pepper

I tablespoon fresh lemon juice

2 cups extra-virgin olive oil

8 large grape leaves

8 slices Greek or other crusty bread

Salad

2 cups fresh arugula, tough stems removed, chilled

I tablespoon fresh lemon juice

3 tablespoons extra-virgin olive oil

Kosher salt and freshly ground black pepper to taste

Herbed Kalamata or other black oil-marinated olives for garnish

Grilled Grape Leaves Filled with Goat Cheese • DOLMATHESTIS SKARA ME TIRI

Prepare a fire in a charcoal grill or preheat a gas grill to high.

In a bowl, stir together the goat cheese, herbs, salt, pepper, lemon juice, and 3 tablespoons of the olive oil.

Spread out 2 of the 8 grape leaves with the long sides overlapping (see facing page). Scoop up a heaping tablespoon of the goat cheese mixture and place it in the middle of the pair of grape leaves. Fold the left long side over the filling, then the right side, and then, starting at the bottom of your leaves, gently roll into a packet with the goat cheese in the center. Repeat with the remaining leaves and goat cheese mixture. Place the stuffed leaves, seam side down, in a shallow dish and pour in the remaining olive oil to cover.

Using tongs, place the packets on the grill. When grill-marked on one side, after about I minute, turn and grill until the leaves are marked on the other side and the cheese is soft, about I minute. Remove from the grill, place on a platter, and cover to keep warm. Brush the bread slices with the olive oil left in the dish, season with salt and pepper to taste, and grill both sides until lightly browned and toasted. Remove from the grill and keep warm.

To assemble the salad, place the arugula in a large salad bowl. Just before serving, dress the arugula lightly with the lemon juice and olive oil, and season with salt and pepper. Place a small mound of arugula in the center of each of 4 individual plates. Place a grilled stuffed packet on top of each mound. Cut each slice of bread in half on the bias and arrange alongside the salads. Garnish with the marinated olives. Serve immediately.

SERVES 4

Rolling Grape Leaves

The trick to stuffing grape leaves, or *dolmathes,* is to overlap two leaves, vein side up. Overlap the leaves so the spines of each leaf are parallel, about 1 $\frac{1}{2}$ to 2 inches apart. Spoon some filling into the center of the leaves, fold the outer edges inward on both sides, and roll tightly into a cylinder. Gently push in the ends to keep the leaves from unfurling.

The sauce for this chicken has layers of flavor, some light and fruity and others deep. The depth comes from *vinocotto*. Also called *saba*, *sapa*, or *mosto cotto*, this deep, rich vinegar is made from fermented grape must. The flavor of *vinocotto* varies slightly from region to region, but it's almost always a good choice when cooking with fresh grapes or other fruit. See Resources on page 190 if you need help finding *vinocotto*.

I first made this dish during the grape harvest in the Napa Valley. Friends brought me clusters of wine grapes, picked 20 minutes earlier, and they were so juicy and flavorful, I was inspired to create a new recipe for chicken around them. Obviously if you live near a vineyard or have friends who make wine, use just-picked wine grapes. For the rest of us, cook with the best grapes you can find. Seedless grapes are good, but choose based on flavor rather than whether or not the grapes have seeds.

This dish goes well with creamy polenta, cous cous, or rice.

Harvest Chicken with *Vinocotto* •
KOTO ME VINOCOTTO

$3/4$ cup extra-virgin olive oil

Four 6-ounce bone-in chicken breasts

$2 3/4$ teaspoons kosher salt

$2 1/8$ teaspoons freshly ground black pepper

2 cups red grapes, halved, seeded if necessary

2 cups green grapes, halved, seeded if necessary

2 teaspoons chopped fresh thyme

$1/2$ small red onion, thinly sliced into half moons

$1/4$ cup *vinocotto*

2 tablespoons champagne vinegar

$3/4$ cup pine nuts, toasted (see note, page 30) (optional)

Preheat the oven to 400°F.

In a large ovenproof skillet, heat $1/2$ cup of the olive oil. Season the chicken breasts with $1/4$ teaspoon salt and $1/8$ teaspoon pepper. Place the breasts in the hot pan, skin side down, and sear until golden brown. Transfer to the oven, leaving the breasts skin side down the entire cooking time to keep the meat on the bottom from drying out. Bake until the juices run clear, 12 to 15 minutes.

Toss together the grapes, thyme, onion, *vinocotto*, the remaining $1/4$ cup olive oil, the champagne vinegar, and the remaining $2 1/2$ teaspoons salt and 2 teaspoons pepper in a large bowl. When the chicken is done, transfer to a serving plate. Spoon the sauce over the warm chicken and top with the toasted pine nuts, if using. Serve immediately.

SERVES **4**

I don't have the biggest sweet tooth in the world, but every so often I *have* to have a *cremosa*. Luscious, light, and creamy, this pretty dessert is everything I want at the end of a meal.

When I first began making this light dessert, I liked it so much I treated myself to one at the end of every workday. People sometimes complain about the long hours a restaurant requires, but I liked that time of the day when the last patron had gone home, the kitchen was sparkling clean once again, and I'd get to have one perfect dessert all to myself. I'd sip my coffee and eat my *cremosa* and feel lucky to be part of a restaurant that I loved.

You can make these custards with a graham cracker base, but I'm a fan of crushed biscotti for my *cremosas*. In summer, I serve this with fresh berries, and through the fall and winter I add a dried fruit conserve or confit.

Champagne brings out the flavor of the strawberries. You can cook with an inexpensive vintage, but I prefer to use a champagne that I'd drink. Invest in a champagne recorker so you can cook with your champagne and also enjoy it the next day when you serve these *cremosas*.

If you already have fancy dessert molds, by all means use them. At my restaurant I make *cremosas* in 3-inch PVC pipes, bought and cut into 1 ½-inch-high rounds for us at the hardware store, then run through the dishwasher. You'll need eight molds or PVC pipe pieces for this recipe.

Make your *cremosas* at least twenty-four hours before serving so the custard has time to chill properly.

Strawberry-Topped Vanilla Custards •
CREMOSAS

Topping

2 cups strawberries, hulled and halved

2 to 4 tablespoons sugar

I or 2 pinches of kosher salt

¼ cup champagne

½ to I teaspoon vanilla

Crust

½ cup roasted hazelnuts
(see note, page 30)

2 cups leftover biscotti, broken
into chunks

¼ cup sugar

½ cup unsalted butter, melted

Filling

1 ¼ cups (10 ounces)
mascarpone cheese

1 ¼ cups sour cream

1 ¼ cups heavy cream

⅔ cup sugar

I vanilla bean

3 to 4 tablespoons cold water

2 ½ teaspoons (I envelope) unflavored
powdered gelatin

Note: Instant-read thermometers are wonderful. They take only seconds to register, are dependable and accurate, and are compact—you can store one in your shirt or apron pocket like a pen.

To make the topping, put the strawberries in a food processor with 2 tablespoons of the sugar, a pinch of salt, the champagne, and ½ teaspoon vanilla. Process to a smooth puree. Refrigerate overnight, then taste the puree just before using. It should have a sharp flavor, softened slightly by the vanilla. Add additional sugar, salt, and vanilla as needed.

To make the crust, combine the biscotti, hazelnuts, and ¼ cup sugar in a food processor and process until finely ground. Slowly add the melted butter; the mixture should come together into a dense crust.

continued

Place eight 3-by-1 1/2-inch ring molds on a parchment paper–lined tray or baking sheet that will fit in your refrigerator. Press 3 tablespoons of the crust mixture evenly into the bottom and up the sides of each mold. Place in the refrigerator to chill while you make the filling.

To make the filling, bring 2 inches of water to a simmer in a large saucepan. When choosing a bowl for the cream mixture, make sure it sits comfortably and snugly in this pan without resting in the water.

Combine the mascarpone, sour cream, heavy cream, and 2/3 cup sugar in a large stainless-steel mixing bowl and whisk to thoroughly combine. With a paring knife, cut a slit down the center of the vanilla bean. With the edge of the knife, force the seam of the bean open, and scrape out the pulp with the tip. Add the vanilla pulp to the cream mixture and mix well.

Place the bowl with the cream mixture over the simmering water. Stir the cream mixture occasionally as the mixture heats. When the cream reaches 150°F on an instant-read thermometer (see note), take the bowl off the water and set aside. Leave the water simmering.

Prepare an ice bath by filling a large bowl halfway with ice and cold water.

Put 1/4 cup of cold water in a small bowl, and sprinkle the gelatin over the water. Let soften for 2 minutes. Hold the bowl over, but not touching, the simmering water used for the cream to melt the gelatin. It should melt in less than a minute. Add the liquefied gelatin to the cream, whisking vigorously. Nestle the bowl with the cream mixture in the cold water bath. Let stand, whisking gently every 10 minutes or so, until the mixture is thickened and cool to the touch, 20 to 25 minutes. It may be necessary to change the ice and water if all the ice melts.

Remove the tray with the biscotti bases from the refrigerator. Ladle approximately 1/2 cup of the cream mixture into each mold. When all of the molds are full, carefully return the tray to the refrigerator. Allow the molds to chill for at least 6 hours, but preferably overnight, until the cream mixture is firmly set.

To unmold, gently run the edge of a small paring knife around the top and bottom inside edges of the mold, releasing the crust and the custard. Hold a plate over the mold and tip it upside down. If the molded custard does not come out easily, rinse a small towel with very hot water (as hot as you can touch without burning yourself) and wring dry. Wrap the cloth around the outside of the mold to help loosen the custard.

When all your *cremosas* are unmolded, transfer to individual plates and top with 2 to 3 tablespoons of the strawberry sauce. Serve immediately.

SERVES **8**

MENU

112 • Summer's First Heirloom Tomatoes
with Fresh Mozzarella

113 • Pan-Seared Halibut
with Sweet Corn Zabaglione

116 • Banana-Coconut Cream Pie

PAN-SEARING A HALIBUT TO GO WITH A SWEET CORN ZABAGLIONE • The flavors of summer—sweet corn and tomatoes—shine in this meal

Every summer, when I first spot heirloom tomatoes in a farmers' market, I have to stop myself from running over to fill up my entire market bag. Picking up that first heirloom of the season and taking a deep breath of its fragrance is almost a religious experience. Even the names of heirloom tomatoes are intoxicating—Brandywine, Black Crimson, Golden Jubilee, Green Zebra, Purple Cherokee.

From those first heirloom tomatoes of the season, I like to make a very simple salad. Great tomatoes, great mozzarella, fresh basil, Vidalia onions, and a little basil oil—that's it, I make this every year, and every year I think it's one of the best salads I've ever tasted.

All of the ingredients used in this meal are similar to heirloom tomatoes—they're at their peak for a short time each year. While I can eat tomatoes and corn on the cob straight up all summer long, it's also nice to taste these flavors in different textures. With right-off-the-cob summer corn, try making a savory zabaglione, perfect beside fish. A zabaglione—called a *sabayon* in France—

is a simple Italian custard made of eggs, sugar, and sweet wine. This recipe does away with the sugar, adds sautéed onions, and makes fresh corn the primary flavor while keeping the same silky, airy texture as a dessert zabaglione.

That's the idea behind all the recipes in this menu. Familiar ingredients put together in ways that make summer's flavors seem new.

This salad celebrates perfect, sun-warmed tomatoes, fresh mozzarella, and basil. It's simple, and few salads taste better. The beauty of this salad is that it works with any off-the-vine summer tomatoes, whether you've picked them from your own garden or from your favorite tomato vendor at a farmers' market. Early Girls aren't considered heirlooms but if that's what's growing in your garden, they're going to be perfect in this salad. Taste tomatoes and choose the most flavorful. The creamy whiteness of the mozzarella and the delicate chiffonade of fresh basil make this salad gorgeous no matter what color tomatoes you use.

Banyuls vinegar, or *Banyuls de vinaigre*, comes from the Pyrenees in the South of France. It's made from Grenache grapes, the ones used for the region's famed dessert wines. This vinegar is considered by some to be the French equivalent of Italian *balsamico*. A basil-infused olive oil adds bright color to the plate and bright flavor to your tomatoes. You can make your own oil (see page 189) or check our Resources on page 190 for suppliers of both Banyuls vinegar and basil-infused olive oil.

I often make my own mozzarella for this salad, but these days you can buy fresh mozzarella or *mozzarella di bufala* that's a pretty good substitute for homemade mozzarella. See Resources on page 190 for two artisans who make fresh mozzarella and will ship it to your door.

Summer's First Heirloom Tomatoes with Fresh Mozzarella

4 large, ripe heirloom tomatoes, cut into $1/4$-inch slices

Kosher salt and freshly ground black pepper to taste

$1/2$ cup Banyuls vinegar

2 medium to large balls fresh mozzarella, cut into $1/4$-inch slices

1 large Vidalia onion, very thinly sliced

6 fresh basil leaves, cut into chiffonade (see note)

6 to 8 tablespoons Basil Oil (page 189) or basil-infused olive oil

Note: To make a chiffonade, stack the basil leaves on top of one another and roll lengthwise into a tight cylinder. Slice crosswise into thin strips.

On each of 4 small plates, place 4 slices of tomato and season lightly with salt and pepper. Drizzle 2 tablespoons of vinegar over each plate of tomato slices, then place a slice of mozzarella on each tomato slice. Ideally, the slice of cheese will be slightly smaller than the round of tomato.

Top the cheese with the onion slices and a small mound of the basil chiffonade. Finish by drizzling the basil oil over the tomatoes and around the edge of each plate.

SERVES **4**

You can't go wrong with halibut. When I want a simple white fish, pan-seared in just a few moments, halibut fillets are my never-fail fish. I think this is one of the simplest meals to make, but when you've placed your seared halibut fillets on the silky, sweet corn zabaglione and topped them with a small mound of arugula and cherry tomatoes, the plate is truly elegant.

Pan-Seared Halibut with Sweet Corn Zabaglione

Prepare the zabaglione as directed.

Preheat the oven to 400°F.

In a sauté pan, heat 1 tablespoon of the olive oil. Season the halibut on both sides, pressing salt and pepper to taste into the fillets. Place the fillets in the hot pan. Brown for about 2 minutes on each side, then transfer to the oven and bake until opaque throughout, 5 to 6 minutes.

While the fish is in the oven, in a bowl, toss together the arugula, tomatoes, onion, and corn. Add the remaining 1 tablespoon olive oil and salt and pepper to taste and mix well.

To serve, divide the zabaglione among 4 warmed individual plates, place a fillet on the zabaglione, and top with some of the arugula and tomato.

SERVES **4**

continued

3 cups Sweet Corn Zabaglione (recipe follows)

2 tablespoons extra-virgin olive oil

Four 6-ounce halibut fillets

Kosher salt and freshly ground black pepper to taste

2 cups fresh arugula, tough stems removed, chilled

1 cup cherry tomatoes, halved

1/2 cup thinly sliced red onion

1/4 cup fresh yellow corn kernels (about 1/2 an ear)

Called a *zabaglione* in Italy and a *sabayon* in France, this silky custard dates back to the sixteenth century and is traditionally a simple combination of eggs, sugar, and dessert wine. This version flavors the custard with corn, sautéed onions, and garlic instead, pureeing and straining the savory mixture before whisking in the egg yolk to thicken it. Still silky and airy, the texture of this zabaglione seems just right with the flavor of fresh summer corn. It's also a lovely complement to chicken or grilled vegetables.

Sweet Corn Zabaglione

In a saucepan, heat the olive oil over high heat and add the onion. Reduce the heat to medium and cook until the onion is translucent, 3 to 4 minutes. Add the corn and garlic and cook until the corn is tender, another 3 to 4 minutes. Add the cream and simmer for 10 minutes. Transfer to a blender and puree the corn mixture until smooth (see note). Strain the puree through a fine-mesh sieve.

Bring 1 inch of water to a simmer in the bottom of a double boiler. Pour the corn puree into a bowl and whisk in the egg yolk. Transfer to the top pan of the double boiler and set over the simmering water. Whisk until thickened, about 10 minutes. Season with salt.

MAKES **3** CUPS

2 tablespoons extra-virgin olive oil

$^1/_2$ cup diced yellow onion

$^1/_2$ cup fresh yellow corn kernels (about 1 ear)

2 cloves garlic, minced

2 cups heavy cream

1 egg yolk

Kosher salt to taste

Note: Always err on the side of caution when blending hot foods. Pour small batches into the blender and hold the lid on tightly while the machine is running.

If you like bananas and coconut, this is your dessert. Creamy coconut filling over banana slices with a whipped topping of cream and mascarpone cheese. I particularly like that all three of the flavors in this pie—banana, mascarpone, and coconut—are layered, so you taste the flavors individually as well as together.

The filling and topping are quite easy to make. Homemade is always better, but if you're running short on time, buy a prebaked 9-inch pie shell and skip making your own pie crust.

Banana-Coconut Cream Pie

Crust

1 1/2 cups all-purpose flour, plus extra for rolling out

1 tablespoon sugar

1/2 teaspoon salt

7 tablespoons chilled unsalted butter, cut into 1/2-inch cubes

1/4 cup vegetable shortening, chilled

2 tablespoons ice water

Vegetable oil for greasing

Filling

1 1/2 cups whole milk

1/2 cup shredded sweetened dried coconut, plus 2 tablespoons

1/3 cup plus 1 tablespoon sugar

2 large egg yolks

2 tablespoons all-purpose flour

1 1/2 teaspoons cornstarch

Pinch of kosher salt

1 1/2 teaspoons vanilla extract

1 tablespoon unsalted butter

1 banana, thinly sliced

Topping

3/4 cup (6 ounces) mascarpone cheese

2 drops vanilla extract

2 tablespoons plus 1 teaspoon confectioners' sugar

3/4 cup heavy cream

To make the crust, combine the 1 1/2 cups flour, the sugar, and the salt in a food processor, and pulse just twice. Add the butter and shortening to the processor and pulse until the mixture forms crumbs the size of peas. Slowly add the water until the crumbs appear moist.

Turn the dough out onto a lightly floured work surface and press into a flat disk. Cover with plastic wrap and let the dough rest in the refrigerator for at least 1 hour. After an hour or more, roll the dough out on a lightly floured work surface into a round 12 inches in diameter and about 1/8 inch thick. Gently pick up the dough and drape it over a 9-inch pie pan. Gently press the dough into the bottom and up the sides of the pan. Trim the edges but leave an extra 1 inch of dough all the way around. Cover with plastic wrap and refrigerate for 1 hour.

Preheat the oven to 425°F.

Lightly oil a sheet of aluminum foil. Fit the foil gently into the chilled pie crust, oil side down. Reduce the oven temperature to 375°F. Fill the pan with pie weights or dried beans over the foil and bake for 20 minutes. Carefully remove the foil and beans, reduce the heat to 325°F, and bake until the shell is golden brown and cooked through, 5 to 8 minutes. Set aside on a wire rack.

To make the filling, heat the milk and the 1/2 cup coconut together in a saucepan just until small bubbles begin to form around the edges of the pan. Take care not to scald the milk. Remove the pan from the heat and let the milk steep for 20 minutes. Strain, pressing the liquid out of the coconut. Discard the coconut. In a bowl, mix the sugar and egg yolks, and then add the 2 tablespoons flour, the cornstarch, and the salt. Reheat the coconut milk gently and temper into the yolk mixture (see note on page 79). Bring to a full boil, stirring constantly. Remove from the heat. Stir in the 2 tablespoons coconut, the vanilla, and the butter.

Arrange the banana slices in the bottom of the prebaked pie crust and immediately pour the filling over the top before the slices can brown. Allow the pie to cool for 2 to 3 hours.

To make the topping, whisk together the mascarpone, vanilla, confectioners' sugar, and $2/3$ cup of the cream until soft peaks form. Add the remaining cream and gently whisk until the cream holds firm peaks. Spoon the cream immediately onto the cooled pie, cut into wedges, and serve.

SERVES **8** TO **10**

MENU

121 • Manila Clams with Fennel-Cured Salami
(ACHIBADES)

122 • Breaded Veal with Tomatoes, Garlic,
and Basil Brown Butter (VITELLO SCALLOPINI)

123 • Fava Bean–Mint Ravioli
with Fava Bean–Mint Pesto

125 • Baked Stuffed Onions (KREMITHES YEMISTA)

127 • Warm Chocolate Ganache over
Coffee Ice Cream (AFFOGATO)

SERVING *ACHIBADES* WITH *VITELLO* (CLAMS AND FENNEL-CURED SALAMI WITH BREADED VEAL) ·
My own version of surf and turf, with an *affogato* for dessert

For this menu, I owe thanks to Michael Chiarello and all the gang at Tra Vigne, who spent one spring helping to create the menu at Postino. Sitting around a table drinking espresso and collaborating on the menu with Michael, Carmen Quagliata, Michael Gyetvan, Mariano Orlando, and Joey Scarpone was plain out fun. Michael introduced me to the idea of clams with sausages, and since then I've created several different versions of this combination of Manila clams and spicy sausage cooked in white wine and chicken stock. I like to serve this particular version before a beautiful *vitello*, or breaded veal served with garlic and tomatoes, which forms the center of this hearty meal. These are sensual dishes, with full, country flavors and enticing textures.

A combination of luscious fava beans and mint fills my plump ravioli and makes up the bright, lively pesto that goes with them. Fava beans are underused. When they're the primary flavor in these ravioli, you get a new appreciation for their sweet, distinctive flavor.

People are often surprised when I serve whole baked onions—they think it's a retro recipe. I think of this dish as a stuffed vegetable, like the Bell Peppers Stuffed with Meat and Rice (page 46) or the Cabbage Leaves (page 79) or the Stuffed Tomatoes (page 80). In Greece, stuffed vegetables have never gone out of style, and I love it when a whole vegetable is stuffed and cooked until the flavors meld. Scooping out a little of the baked onion, finely dicing it, mixing it with cream, and refilling the baked onion gives this country classic a surprisingly elegant finish.

For dessert, place a parfait dish filled with coffee ice cream and warm chocolate sauce in front of guests. Called an *affogato*, this is a sophisticated take on a hot fudge sundae. *Affogato*, which means "drowned," is traditionally ice cream drenched in a cup of steaming hot espresso just before serving. You can do that, too, but I like to mix the espresso with a little liqueur before scooping in the ice cream. This dessert is for my dad, Spiro, lover of coffee, warm chocolate sauce, and ice cream.

When you have great fresh clams, this is the dish to make. Clams and salami aren't a common combination, but it's such a pleasure to alternate between bites of the dense, spicy meat and the silky, sea-tasting clams all in a wine and garlic broth. Once you've tried this, clams without salami may seem a bit lackluster. I particularly like a fennel-cured salami (see Resources, page 190) but you can substitute sausages here, too. If it is summer, throw in some corn for a shot of sweetness.

I like to serve this in a wide, flat bowl, either topped with croutons or served with slices of a hearty bread for soaking up the last of the good wine-garlic broth.

Manila Clams with Fennel-Cured Salami • ACHIBADES

1/4 cup extra-virgin olive oil

2/3 cup sliced fennel-cured salami or other spicy Italian sausage

2 heads of garlic (about 30 cloves), finely chopped

20 to 24 fresh Manila clams

1 cup dry white wine

2/3 cup plus 2 tablespoons Roasted Chicken Stock (page 184)

1 tablespoon plus 1 teaspoon chilled unsalted butter, broken into small pieces

Kosher salt and freshly ground black pepper to taste

6 slices rustic, crusty bread, toasted

3 tablespoons finely chopped fresh Italian (flat-leaf) parsley

1 tablespoon finely chopped fresh oregano

Heat the olive oil in a 12-inch heavy-duty or cast-iron skillet over medium heat and add the salami. Sauté slowly until the salami begins to brown and caramelize slightly on the surface. Add the garlic and cook, stirring, for 10 minutes, until the garlic softens without browning.

Raise the heat slightly. Immediately add the clams and white wine to the pan with the garlic and salami. Bring the wine to a simmer. Scrape the bottom of the pan with a spatula or spoon to deglaze, loosening any browned bits. Add the chicken stock and continue to cook over medium-high heat, bringing the mixture to a steady simmer until all of the clam shells have opened. Reduce the heat to low and discard any clams that have failed to open. Add the bits of butter to the pan and stir them into the mixture. Taste and adjust the seasoning with pepper. Add salt if you like, but sparingly since the salami contributes salt to the flavor of this dish. Spoon into 6 small shallow bowls and top each with 1 slice of the toasted bread and a sprinkling of parsley and oregano. (If you prefer, serve right from the hot skillet, letting guests help themselves to clams, toast, and herbs.)

SERVES **6** AS AN APPETIZER

A basil brown butter sauce, with fresh basil leaves, lemon juice, and garlic, is the perfect accompaniment to thin slices of veal, cooked just until crisp outside and tender inside. This method of cooking takes full advantage of the veal's flavor and tenderness—plus it's quick and easy and makes a sophisticated presentation. Garnish the plate with a few fresh basil leaves and lemon wedges.

I often serve this veal with the Polenta with Fontina and Parmesan (page 70).

Breaded Veal with Tomatoes, Garlic, and Basil Brown Butter • VITELLO SCALLOPINI

Preheat the oven to 200°F.

Pound each piece of veal with a hammer or meat tenderizer until thin. Pour the flour into a shallow dish and season lightly with salt and pepper. Put the eggs in a second shallow dish and the bread crumbs in a third. Dip each piece of veal in the flour, then in the beaten eggs, and then dredge through the bread crumbs. Set the breaded veal aside on a plate.

Arrange the tomato slices in a single layer on a heat-proof platter and dress lightly with the salt, pepper, and vinegar. Heat 3 tablespoons of the olive oil in a 12-inch sauté pan over medium-high heat. Place 2 of the breaded veal slices in the hot oil and brown well, 2 to 3 minutes on each side. Transfer the veal to the platter holding the tomato slices, placing the meat in a layer over the tomatoes. Place the platter in the center of the oven to keep warm. Pour the remaining 3 tablespoons olive oil into the pan, heat, and cook the other 2 veal slices. Transfer as before to the platter in the oven.

Discard the oil from the sauté pan. Add the butter to the pan and melt over medium heat, then cook until it browns slightly. Immediately add the garlic and basil leaves and swirl them in the pan constantly so they do not burn. As the garlic softens and the basil becomes crisp, add the lemon juice to the pan and continue to swirl the ingredients together until well combined. Remove the pan from the heat. Immediately remove the platter with the veal and tomato slices from the oven and pour the sauce over the top of the meat. Sprinkle the cheese on top and garnish with whole basil leaves and lemon wedges.

SERVES 4

Four 4-ounce pieces veal shoulder

1 1/2 to 2 cups all-purpose flour

2 teaspoons salt, plus extra for seasoning the flour

1/4 teaspoon freshly ground black pepper, plus extra for seasoning the flour

2 eggs, lightly beaten

1 to 2 cups dried bread crumbs, preferably panko (see note)

2 large ripe, tomatoes, each cut into 4 slices

1/4 cup red wine vinegar

6 tablespoons olive oil

4 tablespoons unsalted butter

10 to 12 cloves garlic, sliced

12 fresh basil leaves, plus extra for garnish

2 tablespoons fresh lemon juice

2 tablespoons freshly grated pecorino cheese

Lemon wedges for garnish

Note: Japanese panko crumbs, coarser and lighter than ordinary bread crumbs, give a crisper coating to this breaded veal.

While working at Chez Panisse, I once was handed the most beautiful fava beans I've ever seen. Greener than green, these beans had the sweetest flavor. They were practically dewy—you could tell they'd been picked less than a day earlier. See Resources on page 190 for a great resource for fava beans (keeping in mind that good fava beans are available only a short time each year).

When choosing fava beans at a farmers' market or grocery store, look for shells that are plump and bright green. Dark marks or splotches on the shell indicate that the beans inside will be dry and spotty. Shelling beans by yourself is rather tedious, but if you grab a friend and do it together, the task becomes a pleasure. Fava beans require a bit of prep work because you must pull off their husks, blanch the beans, and then skin them again, but the flavor makes the work worthwhile, and if you do this with a partner, it's actually fun. You will shell, blanch, and skin the fava beans for both the filling and the pesto, setting aside half for the pesto.

Because fava beans take some effort, I like to make a lot of these ravioli and freeze them (after handing off half to the partner who helped you shell the beans!). After the ravioli are formed, freeze them on a baking sheet. Once they're frozen, seal tightly in lock-top plastic bags. When you're ready to cook frozen ravioli, before boiling, let the ravioli thaw for 15 to 20 minutes on a parchment-lined baking sheet sprinkled with semolina.

Fava Bean–Mint Ravioli with Fava Bean–Mint Pesto

Dough

2 cups semolina flour, plus extra for dusting

4 teaspoons kosher salt

2 large eggs, at room temperature

1/4 cup whole milk, at room temperature

3 to 7 tablespoons water, at room temperature

4 tablespoons extra-virgin olive oil

Filling

1 cup shelled fava beans, plus 1 cup for the pesto (about 4 pounds whole, unshelled beans total)

1 generous teaspoon kosher salt, plus 1/4 teaspoon

2 cloves garlic, minced

3 tablespoons extra-virgin olive oil

1 tablespoon water, or as needed

1 cup crumbled feta cheese

1 tablespoon finely chopped fresh Italian (flat-leaf) parsley

2 tablespoons finely chopped fresh mint

1/2 cup pine nuts, toasted (see note, page 30)

1/8 teaspoon freshly ground black pepper

To make the dough in a food processor or stand mixer fitted with a paddle attachment, combine the semolina and salt, pulsing or mixing until blended. Add the eggs, milk, 3 tablespoons water, and the olive oil and process until a large ball of smooth dough forms and pulls away from the sides of the bowl. The dough should be smooth and pliable. Add 1 to 4 additional tablespoons of water, if needed. Knead lightly and let the dough rest for 1 hour, covered, in an oiled bowl.

To make the dough by hand, pour the semolina and salt into a large bowl, and make a well in the center. In a separate bowl, beat the eggs lightly with a fork, add the milk, 3 tablespoons water, and the olive oil to the eggs and stir to combine. Pour the egg mixture into the well in the semolina. With a fork or your hands, pull in the flour, gradually incorporating. Add 1 to 4 additional tablespoons of water, if needed. The dough should be smooth and pliable. Knead lightly and let the dough rest for 1 hour, covered, in an oiled bowl.

continued

Turn the dough out onto a lightly floured work surface and knead until smooth. It should not feel sticky. Place the dough in a large bowl, cover with a clean kitchen towel or plastic wrap, and let rest for 1 hour.

Meanwhile, to make the filling, blanch the shelled fava beans to remove the skins: Bring a saucepan half full of water to a boil. Add the kosher salt and the shelled fava beans. Cook until they turn bright green and are tender to the bite, 3 to 4 minutes. Remove from the heat and drain in a colander, rinsing with cold water. As soon as they are cool enough to handle, pinch off the skin by holding a bean between your thumb and forefinger; the skin should slip right off. Skin all the beans, place in a small bowl, and let cool to room temperature.

In the bowl of a food processor, combine 1 cup of the skinned fava beans, the garlic, and olive oil and puree until completely smooth. Add up to 1 tablespoon of water to slightly thin the puree. It should not be runny.

Pesto

1 cup blanched and skinned fava beans

2 tablespoons pine nuts, toasted (see note, page 30)

1 tablespoon fresh mint leaves

6 basil leaves

1 clove garlic, minced

1 teaspoon fresh lemon juice

1 cup extra-virgin olive oil

1 teaspoon kosher salt

$^{1}/_{2}$ teaspoon freshly ground black pepper

$^{1}/_{2}$ cup grated Parmesan cheese

Extra-virgin olive oil for drizzling

$^{1}/_{2}$ cup grated kasseri cheese

Combine the fava bean puree, feta, parsley, mint, and pine nuts in a small bowl. Mix well, and add the remaining $^{1}/_{4}$ teaspoon salt and pepper. Cover and set aside, or refrigerate until ready to use.

Divide the ravioli dough into 4 balls. Lightly flour a rolling pin and the work surface to prevent the dough from sticking. Roll out each ball until paper-thin sheets are formed (you can also use a pasta machine). Place each sheet of dough on a tray or work surface lightly sprinkled with semolina. With a round cookie or biscuit cutter about 3 inches in diameter, cut disks from the sheets of dough. Place a scant $^{1}/_{2}$ teaspoon of filling in the middle of a dough disk, wet a half-circle edge of the disk with water, and fold the disk over to form a half moon. Make sure the edges are sealed tightly. Place the finished ravioli on a large flat tray or baking sheet lightly coated with semolina, keeping them separated so they do not stick to each other. Keep the tray in a cool place until all the ravioli are made and ready to be cooked. If the dough starts to get warm and sticky, the ravioli can be placed in the refrigerator or the freezer for a few minutes until ready to be boiled. (If you'd like to freeze any ravioli, spread them on a pan so they're not touching and place in the freezer.)

To make the pesto, in a blender, combine the remaining 1 cup skinned fava beans, the pine nuts, mint, basil, garlic, lemon juice, olive oil, salt, and pepper and puree until smooth. The pesto should be thick. Taste and adjust the seasoning if necessary. Fold in the Parmesan cheese and set aside.

In a stockpot, bring 5 quarts of water to a boil over high heat. When the water boils, carefully add the ravioli one at a time. Cook in batches, not to exceed 25 ravioli. Cook just until the pasta floats to the top. Remove the pasta gently from the pot with a slotted spoon and place on a warmed platter. Drizzle with olive oil and sprinkle with the kasseri cheese. Serve immediately on warm plates, with pesto on top or alongside.

MAKES ABOUT 100 RAVIOLI; SERVES 8 TO 10

You probably chop onions almost every time you cook, but how often do you look at a whole onion and think about serving it on its own? Baked onions put these hard-working vegetables in the spotlight for a change.

I think baked onions just by themselves are wonderful, but I really like this method of baking, scooping out a little of the baked onion, mixing it with cream, refilling the onion, topping with cheese, and baking until the tops are golden brown.

For this dish, look for smooth, golden yellow onions without any flaws, and don't remove the skin. (This will feel strange, because we skin onions almost automatically, but when you bake them with the skin on, you reserve the juices and the flavor.)

A great side dish with fish, chicken, or beef, this will change how you think about the humble onion. See Resources on page 190 for good kasseri cheese if you have trouble finding this in your cheese market.

4 medium yellow onions, unpeeled

$^1/_2$ cup extra-virgin olive oil

1 $^3/_4$ teaspoons kosher salt

1 teaspoon freshly ground black pepper

1 cup heavy cream

1 $^1/_2$ cups grated kasseri cheese

Baked Stuffed Onions • KREMITHES YEMISTA

Preheat the oven to 400°F.

Cut a $^1/_4$-inch slice from the top of each onion, and cut a very thin slice off the bottom. (Make the bottom slice as thin as possible; this is just to make the onion sit upright in the pan.) Place the onions on a baking sheet and drizzle with the olive oil. Season with $^3/_4$ teaspoon salt and $^1/_2$ teaspoon pepper. Bake until the onions are tender, about 1 $^1/_2$ hours. Remove from the oven and let cool. Leave the oven on.

In a small sauté pan over medium-high heat, reduce the cream until it coats the back of a spoon. Season with the remaining 1 teaspoon salt and $^1/_2$ teaspoon pepper, and set aside.

Remove the skins from the cooled onions and, working from the top, scoop out about one-fourth of each onion, working carefully to keep the shape of the onion intact. Chop the removed portions finely and add to the cream in the saucepan, mixing well. Fill the center of each onion with one-fourth of the onion-cream mixture and divide the cheese among the tops. Return to the oven and bake for 10 minutes.

Remove the onions from the pan with a spatula and transfer to a serving plate.

SERVES 4

This dessert is after-dinner coffee, ice cream, and liqueur all in one parfait dish. It has all the visual appeal of a hot fudge sundae topped with whipped cream and nuts, but the flavors are more sophisticated.

I made this with the help of Terry Paetzold. Terry was my first pastry chef at Postino, and part of the crew that opened my restaurant. She graciously contributed her recipes for ganache and coffee ice cream to this *affogato* recipe.

Think of this dessert in steps. If you're very rushed, you can use store-bought ice cream and chocolate sauce. With just a few extra minutes, you can make Terry's ganache and you'll find it a world away from what you find in a jar. Be sure to use a premium chocolate when making the ganache. I like Callebaut, Scharffen Berger, or Vahlrona (see Resources on page 190).

If you really go the distance and make Terry's coffee ice cream yourself, this dessert soars. I like to serve it in clear glass so you see the layers—either parfait glasses or tall, straight-sided bistro glasses.

Warm Chocolate Ganache over Coffee Ice Cream • AFFOGATO

I cup heavy cream

I teaspoon sugar

I teaspoon vanilla extract

$^1/_2$ cup brewed espresso

$^1/_2$ cup Amaretto

3 cups (twelve $^1/_4$-cup scoops) Terry's Coffee Ice Cream (page 128)

I cup warm Chocolate Ganache (page 128)

$^1/_2$ cup roasted hazelnuts (see note, page 30), roughly chopped

In a bowl, using a whisk or an electric mixer, beat the cream with the sugar and vanilla until soft peaks form.

In the bottom of each of 4 tall dessert glasses, pour 2 tablespoons each of the espresso and Amaretto. Place three $^1/_4$-cup scoops of ice cream into each glass. Pour $^1/_4$ cup of the warm chocolate ganache over each serving of ice cream. Top with two heaping spoonfuls of whipped cream and sprinkle with the hazelnuts. Serve immediately.

SERVES **4**

continued

Chocolate Ganache

Place the chopped chocolate in a bowl. In a saucepan, heat the cream over medium heat until it begins to bubble. Remove from the heat and immediately pour the hot cream over the chopped chocolate. With a whisk, stir the mixture until the chocolate has completely melted and mixed with the cream to form a thick sauce. Use immediately or keep warm over a hot water bath on very low heat until ready to use.

1 cup finely chopped premium bittersweet chocolate

$^1/_2$ cup heavy cream

MAKES 1 CUP

Terry's Coffee Ice Cream

Place the whole coffee beans in a small locktop bag and close tightly. With a rolling pin, crush the beans into coarse pieces. Pour the crushed beans into a saucepan with the milk, $^1/_2$ cup of the sugar, and 1 cup of the cream. Place the saucepan over medium heat and slowly bring the milk mixture to a simmer, stirring to dissolve the sugar. Remove from heat as soon as bubbles break the surface. Allow the coffee beans to steep in the heated milk and cream for at least 1 hour. Strain the mixture into a saucepan and set aside. Discard the coffee beans.

1 cup whole Italian-roast coffee beans

2 cups whole milk

1 $^1/_4$ cups sugar

2 cups heavy cream

8 large egg yolks

Have ready a large bowl filled with ice water. In another bowl, with an electric mixer, whisk the egg yolks with the remaining $^3/_4$ cup sugar until the mixture becomes pale yellow and forms a ribbon. Reheat the espresso-flavored milk mixture, bringing it to a simmer. Immediately remove it from the heat, and with the mixer on low speed, slowly ladle about $^1/_2$ cup of the hot milk mixture into the beaten eggs and sugar (see note, page 79). While mixing, add the remaining hot milk mixture in a slow, steady stream until incorporated. Scrape the mixture from the sides and the bottom of the bowl, mix well, and pour through a sieve into another bowl. Add the remaining 1 cup cold cream and stir well to combine thoroughly. Place in the ice bath. Stir until the mixture has completely cooled. Transfer the mixture to a covered container and chill thoroughly in the refrigerator for at least 2 hours or until ready to churn.

Follow the manufacturer's directions for your ice-cream maker for churning and freezing. After churning the ice cream, cover tightly and place in the freezer to set for at least 1 hour or until ready to serve.

MAKES 1 $^1/_2$ QUARTS

MENU

133 • Crab and Avocado "Sandwiches"
with Mango Coulis

134 • Prawns in Grappa Cream Sauce
with Salsa Rosa

136 • Split Lobster Stuffed
with Crabmeat (ASTAKOS SPIROS)

137 • Spicy Broccoli Rabe

139 • Fresh Fruit Tart

FISHING FOR COMPLIMENTS AT MY SEAFOOD FEST ·
Cooking just about every type of seafood and pulling out all the stops

When my dad was growing up, fish was an everyday staple, and not cause for much excitement. Lobsters, shrimp, and crab on the other hand—these were rarities, and my father adored them. During my childhood, these foods meant special occasions, and special occasions often meant dinner at one of the restaurants of my godfather, Peter J. Costas, known to my family as Taki.

Taki owned several restaurants in Jackson. The fanciest was the Continental, an old-style restaurant with big leather booths that you sank into when you sat down. The Continental was my favorite place in the world to eat because Taki would come out to the dining room, take me by the hand into the kitchen, and lift me up onto the counter where I'd sit talking to the cooks. I remember them asking me, "What do you want to eat; we'll cook you anything you like." When you're five years old, sitting in an enormous kitchen with three people asking what they can cook for you, of course you develop a fondness for restaurant kitchens.

Before my parents came to see my restaurant in California for the first time, one of the best fish vendors in Northern California called me to say he had a really great selection of shellfish. The timing was perfect. Gorgeous crab, prawns, and lobster—my dad's favorites—would all be offered on the same menu.

I set to work creating seafood for special occasions. While I was testing some new ideas, some friends of mine dropped by the restaurant. I set out a dish of the prawns in a grappa cream sauce with a salsa rosa. I went back into the kitchen and was there for only a few minutes when the server came in and said my friends were asking for more— and this was a good-sized dish of prawns. I went out into the restaurant and my friends were practically thumping their utensils on the table, demanding another plateful,

so I ran back into the kitchen and quickly made another batch.

I knew the crab and avocado "sandwiches"—crab cakes filled with avocado salsa, resting on a bright mango coulis—might be a little too *nouvelle cuisine* for my parents, but the combination was too appealing to pass up. On the other hand, the lobster, stuffed with crabmeat, was a surefire hit, and I was pretty sure the prawns would get a thumbs-up. As far as my parents are concerned, you can't go wrong with lobster and prawns.

A fruit tart made with lush, ripe mangos, kiwis, and berries provided just the right note of color and freshness at the meal's end.

Bottom line: My parents loved their meal at my restaurant, and so did the other patrons. My friends still come over to my place requesting prawns in grappa cream sauce. The seafood fest became a regular occurrence.

The best part of having my parents come to my restaurant was the kindness and generosity shown by the restaurant's wait staff. The other patrons were trying to figure out who these important people were, with five or six waiters attending their every move. It doesn't matter if you're the president or even Brad Pitt and Jennifer Aniston—nobody is treated better in a restaurant than the chef's family.

2 cups canola oil

$1/2$ pound fresh Maine or Dungeness lump crabmeat

3 tablespoons finely chopped red onion

2 tablespoons thinly sliced scallions

$1 1/2$ tablespoons finely diced red bell pepper

$1/4$ cup best-quality mayonnaise or Tangerine Aioli (page 94)

1 tablespoon Tabasco or other hot pepper sauce

$1 1/4$ cups dried bread crumbs, preferably panko crumbs (see note, page 122)

2 tablespoons fresh lemon juice

$1 1/2$ tablespoons Worcestershire sauce

1 cup all-purpose flour

$1/2$ teaspoon salt

$1/4$ teaspoon freshly ground black pepper

1 egg, lightly beaten

Avocado Salsa

2 large avocados, pitted, peeled, and cut into chunks

2 tablespoons fresh lime juice

1 tablespoon chopped fresh cilantro, plus whole sprigs for garnish

2 tablespoons finely diced red onion

1 tablespoon extra-virgin olive oil

$1/4$ teaspoon kosher salt

Mango Coulis

2 mangos, cut into chunks (see note)

$1 1/2$ to 2 cups water

1 teaspoon confectioners' sugar

Don't look for bread in these sandwiches. They're classic crab cakes split in half, filled with a cool, tangy avocado salsa, and placed in a bright pool of mango coulis. The avocado complements the warm, rich crab, and the coulis adds a tropical touch.

Crab and Avocado "Sandwiches" with Mango Coulis

In a deep sauté pan, heat 1 cup of the canola oil over high heat until a deep-frying or candy thermometer reads 375°F. In a bowl, combine the crabmeat, onion, scallions, bell pepper, mayonnaise, Tabasco, $1/4$ cup of the bread crumbs, the lemon juice, and Worcestershire sauce. Mix until fully incorporated. Form into cakes about 3 inches in diameter and $3/4$ inch thick. Place the flour on a plate, and stir in the salt and pepper. Place the beaten egg in a bowl and the remaining 1 cup bread crumbs on another plate. Dredge each crab cake in the flour, then in the egg, and then in the bread crumbs. Lay the cakes in the oil and panfry until each cake has a nice brown crust on both sides, 5 to 6 minutes total. Transfer to paper towels to drain.

To make the salsa, combine all the ingredients in a bowl, mixing gently. I like this to have bright green chunks of avocado (which the lime juice keeps from turning brown), rather than to be a smooth guacamole concoction. Refrigerate the salsa until ready to use.

To make the mango coulis, place the mango chunks in blender with $1 1/2$ cups water and the confectioners' sugar. Process until smooth. If the mixture is too thick, pour in another $1/4$ cup of water, blend, and again check the consistency, adding up to $1/4$ cup more water if necessary. Refrigerate the coulis until ready to use.

To serve, spoon coulis into the center of individual plates in a small pool. Slice each crab cake in half to make 2 round pieces and lay the bottoms in the puree. Spoon some avocado salsa on top of each and place the top portions of the crab cakes over the salsa like a sandwich. Top with a small amount of salsa and garnish with cilantro sprigs.

SERVES **4** TO **6**

Note: I've found the easiest way to cut a mango is to cut a fat slice off each flat side, moving your knife parallel to the broad side of the pit inside. You'll have mango thirds, with the two outer thirds free of the pit. With a sharp knife cut a checkerboard pattern in the flesh of the two outer thirds, slicing first in one direction and then the other without cutting through the skin. Then flip the mango piece inside out so the cut side is curving outward. You'll find the crosshatching you've done makes the chunks stand out so they're easy to cut away from the skin with a knife.

I like to try different liquors and liqueurs in my cooking, and I'm especially interested in experimenting with the spirits from the cuisine that I'm working in. So I'll marinate fajitas in tequila, or cook my Spicy Gypsy Mussels (page 101) with ouzo. For these Italian-style prawns, I deglaze the pan with grappa, a potent brandylike eau de vie made from the grape residue left after wine-making. I finish the sauce with a bright, smooth red salsa rosa. Made from roasted tomatoes and red bell peppers, salsa rosa has a flavor as vivid as its color. These prawns have been a great hit both in my restaurant and at parties at home.

Calabrian chilies have an appealing depth of flavor, especially when they're roasted. You can buy whole chilies from a specialty market, but I find the easiest way to cook with this Italian favorite is to buy jars of chilies packed in oil (see Resources on page 190).

I tend to make my salsa rosa fairly spicy. If you'd like a milder version, add just two or three roasted chilies, blend the mixture, and taste to see if you'd like it a little spicier. Add roasted chilies two or three at a time, blending after each addition, until this sauce is just as hot as you like it.

Prawns in Grappa Cream Sauce with Salsa Rosa

I tablespoon olive oil

I clove garlic, sliced

20 prawns (16 to 20 per pound), cleaned and deveined

$1/4$ teaspoon kosher salt

$1/8$ teaspoon freshly ground black pepper

I tablespoon plus I $1/2$ teaspoons basil, coarsely chopped, plus whole leaves for garnish

2 tablespoons grappa

$3/4$ cup heavy cream

20 cherry tomatoes, halved

2 tablespoons Salsa Rosa (facing page)

In a sauté pan, heat the olive oil. Add the garlic and cook until barely golden brown. Add the prawns and sear in the hot oil and garlic. Stir in the salt, pepper, and chopped basil. When the prawns are pink, add the grappa and scrape the bottom of the pan with a spatula or spoon to deglaze, loosening any browned bits. Heat for I minute to cook off the alcohol.

Add the cream, tomatoes, and salsa rosa. Mix well. Let the cream reduce for 3 to 4 minutes. Taste and adjust the seasoning. Serve hot, garnishing the plates with basil leaves.

SERVES **4**

This recipe makes a lot of Salsa Rosa, but it keeps well in the freezer for up to 3 to 4 weeks. Use this salsa to add color and spice to many seafood, chicken, or pasta dishes.

Salsa Rosa

Preheat the broiler.

Heat a large, dry cast-iron or heavy-duty skillet over medium-high heat. Place the whole tomatoes in the hot skillet, being careful not to crowd them. Turning them occasionally with tongs, blacken as much as possible on all sides. When blackened all the way around, remove the tomatoes from the skillet and place on a wire rack to cool. Repeat with the remaining tomatoes. When the tomatoes are cool enough to handle, remove the stem ends and the skins with a small paring knife. The skins should almost slide off. Place the roasted tomatoes in a bowl and set aside, or cover and refrigerate until ready to use.

Place the whole bell peppers on a baking sheet and place under the broiler. Blacken as evenly as possible on all sides, turning every 4 to 5 minutes with long-handled tongs or a fork. When blackened all the way around, remove the peppers from the broiler. Place them in a plastic bag and close it tightly. Allow them to cool in the bag for 20 to 30 minutes. Remove the cooled peppers from the bag. With a sharp paring knife, peel the softened skins away and remove the stem, seeds, and ribs from each pepper. Place the skinned and cleaned roasted pepper pieces in a bowl and set aside or cover and refrigerate until ready to use.

(If you don't have Calabrian chilies, roast, skin, and seed the fresh red chilies the same way you roasted the red bell peppers, above.)

Put the roasted tomatoes, roasted red bell peppers, and roasted chilies in a food processor or blender. Add the vinegar, salt, and pepper and pulse the mixture until smooth. Taste and adjust the seasoning. Pour the tomato mixture through a chinois or a large fine-mesh strainer over a large bowl. Transfer the strained sauce to a container, cover, and refrigerate to chill until ready to use.

2 pounds plum (Roma) tomatoes

2 pounds red bell peppers

2 tablespoons chopped roasted oil-packed Calabrian chilies (see Resources, page 190) or 2 or 3 small fresh red chilies

$^1/_3$ cup sherry vinegar

$^1/_2$ teaspoon kosher salt

Freshly ground black pepper to taste

MAKES 5 $^1/_2$ CUPS

When I taste this lobster stuffed with crab, I have to side with my dad when he says food doesn't get more extravagant than this.

Buy lobsters live and keep them in a cool or refrigerated spot until cooking time. I store mine in a small cardboard box with a few pieces of damp newspaper on top to keep them moist. This recipe calls for big lobsters. Check with your seafood vendor a week before you plan to make these. Often, large lobster can be ordered with as little as twenty-four hours' notice.

I think the best bread crumbs are made from stale bread (avoid presliced white bread if you can). Just pulse the bread quickly in a food processor, spread the crumbs over a baking sheet, and toast lightly in a 350°F oven for 2 to 3 minutes.

Split Lobster Stuffed with Crabmeat •
ASTAKOS SPIROS

Kosher salt as needed

Two live lobsters, about 2 1/2 pounds each

1/2 pound fresh lump crabmeat

1/4 cup best-quality mayonnaise

1 small egg

1 cup dried bread crumbs

2 tablespoons scallions, chopped

2 tablespoons fresh basil, finely chopped

1 large pinch of red pepper flakes

1 tablespoon chopped fresh dill, plus whole dill sprigs for garnish

1/2 teaspoon kosher salt

1/8 teaspoon freshly ground black pepper

1/4 cup fresh lemon juice

1/2 cup extra-virgin olive oil

Lemon wedges for serving

Bring a very large stockpot of water to a boil, adding 1 tablespoon of salt for every 2 quarts of water. Immerse the lobsters quickly, head first, into the boiling water and cook until the shell turns bright orange, 8 to 10 minutes. Remove the lobsters from the pot with large tongs, place them on a platter, and let cool.

In a small bowl, mix together the crabmeat, mayonnaise, egg, 3/4 cup of the bread crumbs, the scallions, basil, red pepper flakes, chopped dill, salt, and pepper. Set aside. Combine the lemon juice and olive oil in another small bowl and set aside.

Preheat the oven to 375°F.

When the lobsters are cool enough to handle, cut each in half lengthwise. Remove the entire inside of the head and rinse. Place the lobster halves on a baking sheet, meat side up, and fill the head cavity with the crabmeat stuffing. Sprinkle with the remaining 1/4 cup bread crumbs. Bake until the filling is hot and the bread crumbs have browned lightly, 15 to 20 minutes. Place on a large warmed platter garnished with dill sprigs and lemon wedges, and serve immediately. Transfer the lemon juice mixture to small serving bowls for dipping the succulent lobster meat.

SERVES 4

A staple in southern Italy, broccoli rabe is one of those greens that's very good for you but slightly bitter. A quick blanching before stir-frying takes care of most of the bitterness. Extremely easy to make, flavored with thin slices of garlic and a hint of red pepper flakes, these clean-tasting, spicy greens complement every one of the seafood dishes in this menu.

Spicy Broccoli Rabe

Bring a large saucepan three-fourths full of salted water to a boil. Add the chopped broccoli rabe and blanch for 3 minutes. Drain and set aside.

8 cups coarsely chopped broccoli rabe

2 tablespoons extra-virgin olive oil

6 cloves garlic, sliced

$1/4$ teaspoon kosher salt

$1/8$ teaspoon freshly ground black pepper

$1/8$ teaspoon red pepper flakes

I lemon, cut into quarters

Heat the olive oil in a sauté pan. Cook the garlic until golden brown, 2 to 3 minutes. Add the blanched rabe and season with the salt, pepper, and red pepper flakes. Give the rabe a squeeze of lemon juice and serve with the lemon quarters.

SERVES **4** TO **6**

Dough

1 3/4 cups all-purpose flour

1/4 cup sugar

1/4 teaspoon salt

10 tablespoons chilled unsalted butter, cut into pieces

1 large egg yolk

3 tablespoons cold water

vegetable oil for greasing

Pastry Cream

3 large egg yolks, lightly beaten

1/2 cup sugar

2 tablespoons cornstarch

1 cup whole milk

1/2 vanilla bean, split lengthwise

2/3 cup apricot preserves

2 teaspoons Cointreau or Grand Marnier (optional)

3 kiwis, peeled and thinly sliced

1 ripe mango, pitted, peeled, and thinly sliced (see note, page 133)

1/4 fresh pineapple, peeled, cored, and thinly sliced

10 blackberries

10 raspberries

10 strawberries, thinly sliced

Note: To speed up the chilling process, make an ice bath by filling a large bowl with ice and water. Place the bowl of pastry cream in the ice bath and stir it about every 5 minutes until thoroughly chilled. Use immediately or store in the refrigerator.

A buttery tart crust topped with cool pastry cream and a variety of shining jewel-colored fruit is always a crowd-pleaser, welcome at every occasion. Tropical fruits—mangoes, kiwis, and pineapple—taste especially good to me after seafood.

You can use any fruit you like for this tart. If you want to make it with just blueberries and strawberries for the Fourth of July, go for it. Just be sure whatever fruit you use is picture-perfect and ripe.

Fresh Fruit Tart

To make the dough, in a food processor fitted with the metal blade, combine the flour, sugar, and salt and pulse just a few seconds to blend. Add the chilled butter pieces and process for 1 minute or less, until mixture is the consistency of a coarse meal. Whisk together the egg yolk and water in a small bowl. Pour the egg mixture into the feed tube of the processor. As the egg mixture moistens the dry ingredients, pulse steadily until the dough gathers into a ball and all of the liquid is incorporated. Remove the dough from the processor, flatten into a disk about 1-inch thick, and wrap in plastic. Refrigerate for 1 hour.

Preheat the oven to 375°F.

With a rolling pin, roll out the dough on a lightly floured work surface into a 14-inch round. Drape over an 11-inch round tart pan with a removable bottom and gently push the dough into the bottom and up the sides of the pan. Trim the top edge of the tart by running the rolling pin over the edge of the pan. Cover with plastic wrap and chill for at least 15 minutes. Lightly oil a sheet of aluminum foil. Fit the foil gently into the chilled crust, oil side down. Fill the pan with pie weights or dried beans over the foil and bake until the sides of the crust are set, about 15 minutes. Remove the foil and beans. Continue to bake until the crust is golden, about 5 to 8 minutes longer, piercing it with a fork if bubbles form. Transfer to a wire rack and let cool completely.

To make the pastry cream, with a whisk or an electric mixer, beat the egg yolks with the sugar and cornstarch in a bowl until thick and well blended. Set aside. Place the milk in a heavy saucepan over medium heat. Scrape the seeds from the vanilla bean with the tip of a knife and add to the milk, along with the scraped bean husk. Bring to a simmer and remove from the heat. Slowly add a few spoonfuls of the hot milk into the yolk and sugar mixture, whisking vigorously to temper the eggs (see note, page 79). Gradually add the remaining hot milk mixture, mixing constantly. Return the mixture to the saucepan and whisk over medium heat until it thickens and comes to a simmer. Simmer for 1 minute, stirring all the while. Pour the pastry cream into a clean bowl. Press plastic wrap onto the surface to prevent a skin from forming and

continued

refrigerate for 3 hours, or until thoroughly chilled. (If you're short on time, see note on page 139.)

To make the tart's glaze: Put the apricot preserves in a small, heavy saucepan. Stir over low heat until melted. Transfer to a food processor and puree until smooth. Strain the puree through a fine-mesh sieve into a bowl.

To assemble the tart, with a pastry brush, apply about one-third of the strained apricot jelly evenly over the bottom surface of the prebaked crust. Remove the pastry cream from the refrigerator and soften by mixing with a spoon. Taste the pastry cream, and if you like, add the Cointreau. Spread all of the pastry cream evenly over the brushed layer of jelly. Arrange the cut fruit and berries decoratively over the pastry cream, alternating colors and textures. Rewarm the remaining apricot puree and brush lightly over the fruit. Chill the tart until ready to serve.

SERVES **8** TO **10**

MENU

145 • Salt-Roasted Beets, Arugula,
and Endive Salad (PANTZARIA SALATA)

146 • Muscovy Duck Breasts
with Black Rice,
Pistachios, and Orange

148 • Prunes and Armagnac with Vanilla Gelato
(VANILA PAGATO ME THAMASKINO KE ARMAGNAC)

COMBINING A VELVETY DUCK BREAST WITH EXOTIC BLACK RICE • Adding pistachios and oranges to black rice makes this my favorite restaurant meal

Some meals come together perfectly. This is one of those meals. I think the combination of textures and colors here is simply outstanding—the velvety duck breast, the green, crunchy pistachios, the bright juicy oranges, all on a bed of exotic black rice. This is a true restaurant meal, one with ingredients not often found in a home kitchen. Because it's one of my favorites at the restaurant, I wanted to make this meal accessible to home cooks.

I love the flavor and deep, jewel-toned colors of beets, and I think salt-roasting best preserves both flavor and color. Tossed in a white wine vinaigrette with shallots, these beets rest on a bed of arugula and endive.

Prunes may be the frumpiest of fruits, but when they're warmed and plumped in Armagnac and spooned over vanilla gelato these are nothing short of elegant. I was never a big prune fan until I tasted this dessert and was just amazed by how good it is. I like to think of the Armagnac as a sort of fairy godmother for the Cinderella prunes. You take these humble, almost laughably stodgy dried fruits and with a wave of your wooden spoon, they're transformed into the belle of the ball. This dessert is the happy ending for the meal.

I to 2 cups kosher salt

3 large beets (golden or chiogga beets), washed but not peeled or trimmed

$1/2$ cup roasted pistachios, almonds, or hazelnuts (see note, page 30), roughly chopped

2 endives

Vinaigrette

$1/2$ cup white wine vinegar, white balsamic vinegar, or champagne vinegar

$1 1/4$ cups light olive oil

I medium shallot, minced

I tablespoon finely chopped fresh thyme

I teaspoon kosher salt

$1/4$ teaspoon freshly ground black pepper

Pinch of sugar

4 cups fresh arugula, tough stems removed, chilled

$1/2$ teaspoon kosher salt for tossing

$1/2$ teaspoon freshly ground pepper for tossing

$1/2$ cup Parmesan cheese shavings (see note)

Note: To make shavings from Parmesan or other hard cheeses, use a cheese shaver, vegetable peeler, or sharp knife to slice paper-thin wide curls.

This recipe takes full advantage of a beet's beautiful color and flavor by salt roasting. This is a great method when you want to experiment with the flavor of various beets. You can use small beets, too, but roast them for much less time, tending the beets carefully and pulling them from the oven when a fork slides in easily.

Salt-Roasted Beets, Arugula, and Endive Salad • PANTZARIA SALATA

Preheat the oven to 350°F.

Spread enough kosher salt to cover the bottom of a small baking dish and rest the beets upright on the salt. Roast until tender when pierced with a knife, about $1 1/2$ hours. Give the beets at least 30 minutes to cool. Raise the oven temperature to 400°F.

Wearing gloves or holding a piece of plastic wrap or aluminum foil to protect your fingers, cut off the beets' stems and peel each beet. Cut the beets in half, then cut into $1/2$-inch slices and give the beets a medium dice by cutting in the opposite direction. Set aside.

Spread the pistachios on a baking sheet and toast in the oven, tossing once, until fragrant and lightly golden, about 15 minutes. Remove from the baking sheet immediately and set aside.

Trim the stem ends of the endives and cut each head in half. Separate the leaves for each half, then stack them again to form half a head of endive. Set aside.

To make the vinaigrette, combine all of the ingredients. Stir in the cooled nuts.

I like to dress each salad separately. For each salad, set aside $1/2$ cup beets, I cup arugula, and half of each endive. In a bowl, combine $1/2$ cup of the vinaigrette, $1/8$ teaspoon salt, and $1/8$ teaspoon pepper. Toss each component of the salad— arugula, endive, and beets—separately in the seasoned vinaigrette, making sure to toss the beets last. Arrange the vegetables on an individual plate. Rinse the bowl and repeat to assemble the remaining 3 salads.

Top each salad with 2 tablespoons of shaved Parmesan cheese. Serve immediately.

SERVES 4

A perfect Muscovy duck resting on a bed of elegant dark rice studded with bright orange segments and green pistachios—this combination is memorable. See Resources on page 190 for great Muscovy duck.

Muscovy Duck Breasts with Black Rice, Pistachios, and Orange

4 tablespoons extra-virgin olive oil

2 small yellow onions, finely diced

$\frac{1}{2}$ cup dry white wine

1 cup black rice (see note) or wild rice

1 $\frac{1}{2}$ cups Roasted Chicken Stock (page 184)

Two 10-ounce boneless duck breast halves or one 16-ounce breast

Kosher salt and freshly ground black pepper to taste

$\frac{1}{2}$ cup pistachios

Sauce

1 $\frac{1}{2}$ cups Roasted Chicken Stock (page 184)

6 tablespoons unsalted butter

20 to 24 orange segments, membrane, seeds, and pith removed

Kosher salt and freshly ground black pepper to taste

3 tablespoons finely chopped chives

Note: Black rice can be difficult to find, so you can substitute wild rice or Thai rice if necessary. If you can find black rice, you'll be pleased with its color and nutty flavor. It changes the tone of the meal just by how unusual it looks on the plate. See Resources, page 190.

Preheat the oven to 400°F.

In a saucepan, heat 2 tablespoons of the olive oil over medium-high heat. Add the onions and cook until translucent, 3 to 4 minutes. Add the wine and cook to reduce by half. Add the rice, stirring until each grain is coated. Add the 1 $\frac{1}{2}$ cups stock and bring to a boil. Reduce the heat to low and continue cooking the rice at a low simmer, uncovered, for 35 minutes. Cover, and cook until the rice is tender, about 10 minutes longer. Take the rice off the heat before it becomes mushy. Set the rice aside and cover to keep warm.

While the rice is cooking, season the duck breast with salt and pepper to taste. Set aside. Heat the remaining 2 tablespoons of olive oil in an ovenproof sauté pan over medium-high heat. Place 1 duck breast, skin side down, in the hot pan, searing it until the skin is golden brown, approximately 4 minutes. (Ideally, you would cook one or two duck breasts in separate pans at the same time.) Transfer the pan to the middle shelf of the oven and roast the duck, still skin side down, for about 10 to 12 more minutes. The duck should be done when the flesh feels slightly firm to the touch. Remove the duck from the oven and transfer to a carving board to rest for at least 10 minutes.

On a baking sheet, spread out the pistachios and place in the oven. Bake until the nuts are light brown, about 4 to 5 minutes. Remove from the oven and let cool. Rough chop the nuts and set aside until ready to use.

To make the sauce, in a saucepan, bring the 1 $\frac{1}{2}$ cups chicken stock to a boil over medium heat and cook to reduce by half. Reduce the heat to low, add the butter, and swirl into the reduced stock until the sauce has thickened slightly. Add the orange segments, gently tossing them in the sauce, and season lightly with salt and pepper. Taste and adjust the seasoning. Set aside on very low heat to keep warm.

To serve, spoon a nice mound of rice in the middle of each individual warmed plate. Slice the duck on the bias into thin slices and divide among the plates, overlapping the slices in a fan around the rice. Spoon the warm orange sauce over the duck and rice and sprinkle with the toasted pistachios. Garnish with the chives and serve immediately.

SERVES **2 TO 4**

As simple and easy to make as it is elegant, this sauce makes vanilla gelato seem lavish. The secret is Armagnac, a dry French brandy that transforms plain prunes into an extravagant sauce. Be sure to make this prune sauce at least one week before you plan to serve it. This sauce is also a nice gift for friends when stored in pretty jars—but please do be sure to keep it refrigerated.

Prunes and Armagnac with Vanilla Gelato ⋆
VANILA PAGATO ME THAMASKINO KE ARMAGNAC

$^3/_4$ cup water

3 tablespoons firmly packed brown sugar

1 pound large pitted prunes

$^1/_2$ cup Armagnac, or more to taste

2 cups Vanilla Gelato (recipe follows)

In a nonaluminum saucepan, combine the water and brown sugar. Bring to a boil over medium-high heat, stirring until the sugar dissolves.

Reduce the heat to medium and add the prunes to the pan with the syrup. Simmer for 3 to 4 minutes. Set aside and let cool completely, then stir in the Armagnac. Taste it and decide if you'd like more Armagnac. Pour into a jar and close tightly. Refrigerate for at least 1 week before serving.

Refrigerated, the prunes will keep indefinitely. When ready to serve, warm the prunes and spoon over the vanilla gelato.

SERVES 4 TO 6

Vanilla Gelato

In a saucepan, heat the milk over medium-low heat until you see small bubbles around the edges. Remove from the heat.

Whisk the sugar and egg yolks together in a large bowl and add just a few tablespoons of the hot milk, whisking vigorously to temper the eggs (see note, page 79). Slowly add the rest of the warm milk, whisking steadily until all the milk has been added.

2 cups whole milk

$^1/_2$ cup sugar

4 egg yolks

2 teaspoons vanilla extract

In a clean saucepan, cook the egg mixture over medium-low heat, stirring with a wooden spoon or spatula. The mixture is done when the custard is thick enough to coat the back of a spoon and leaves a path with clean edges when you run your finger along the spoon's back.

Remove from the heat and pour the custard through a chinois or fine-mesh sieve placed over a clean bowl. After draining, stir in the vanilla extract. Refrigerate the mixture for at least 1 hour or until thoroughly chilled.

Follow the manufacturer's directions for your gelato or ice-cream maker for churning and freezing. After churning the gelato, cover tightly and place in the freezer to set for at least 3 hours, or until ready to serve.

MAKES 2 CUPS

My Kitchen at

HOME

For years I worked a hundred hours a week in my restaurant kitchen, and meals at home were an afterthought—made quickly, no frills, and eaten in a hurry. This pace went against everything I learned in my parents' home. When my mom and dad came home from work and sat down to dinner, they were ready to stay at the table and visit with their family. I remember my mom very purposefully loading up the table with everything we could possibly need—from extra bowls of *tzatziki* (page 58) to platters of feta cheese and even dessert—so once she sat down to dinner she could stay seated. One of the things I love most about my family is that we all stay around the table, laughing and talking even after the dessert is long gone.

Watching my Greek relatives celebrate every single meal, stocking the table with bottles of ouzo and *tsiporo*, and staying at the table for hours, reminded me of those childhood dinners. When I returned from my trip to Greece, I set out to change how I cooked at home.

My all-grill dinner reflects this change of heart. I was cooking dinner for friends in Oakland, California, one 99-degree afternoon. All my guests were chatting and laughing outside, enjoying the first breeze of the day, while I raced around a hot kitchen by myself. I ran outside to deliver more appetizers and realized I was missing my own party. I caught myself, thought about those meals in Greece, thought about sitting at the table outside just a few yards from my uncle Yiorgios while he cooked a whole goat, and I came up with plan B. Five minutes later, all of my friends had a hold on my big wooden dining table, and we somehow maneuvered it out through my narrow patio door. I lit the grill and cooked everything I possibly could over the fire with all my friends at the table beside me while I cooked. And, I'm proud to say, I just left any dishes that couldn't be cooked outdoors off the menu. For me, my all-grill menu symbolizes the best of both worlds—cooking for people, which I love, and joining in my own party.

These days I let the ingredients tell me when to cook. The gorgeous tomatoes of midsummer mean it's time for *domatokeftethes*, delicate little tomato croquettes that travel well enough to pack up for a picnic. Lush, ripe watermelon is my signal to make my signature watermelon, feta, and mint salad—completely refreshing and like no melon salad you've ever had.

And I try to slow down the pace. In Greece, life stops for meals, and time at the table is never rushed. We Americans are too ready to eat on the run, and we're missing out. My favorite way to eat, bringing out lots of *mezes*, or little plates, lets friends relax while they taste and talk and taste some more.

That's the heart of Greek cooking: Put all your food on the table, bring out the spirits, and don't even think about getting up until everybody is filled up with good food and the company of friends.

MENU

155 • Tomato Croquettes with Cucumber Yogurt
(DOMATOKEFTETHES ME TZATZIKI)

156 • Lamb-and-Cheese-Stuffed Sandwiches
(ARNI KAI MYZITHRA SKOPELOS)

158 • Watermelon, Feta,
and Mint Salad

PACKING UP A WINE COUNTRY/TAILGATE PARTY
PICNIC • Cooking both hearty and delicate foods for alfresco meals

There are two kinds of picnics. There's the delicate repast, where
you bring along some olives, some cheeses, and a bottle of wine in
a pretty little basket. And then there's the hearty picnic, the kind
where you offer people hefty slices of a stuffed sandwich filled
with juicy lamb and melting cheese—and their faces light up
because they were expecting just cheese and olives.

Definitely hearty, this menu centers around a big, warm
sandwich of lamb sirloin and Myzithra cheese, garlic,
and tomatoes, all cooked inside a hollowed-out loaf of
country bread, then cut into wide slices. As someone
who's brought both kinds of picnics, I can tell you the
response you get when you hold out a piece of this sandwich will make you glad you didn't go for the cheese-
and-olives option. This sandwich satisfies in a big way.

And because I like the idea of a delicate repast served
alongside a big hunk of a sandwich, I accompany it with
croquettes made out of fresh summer tomatoes and
topped with cool Cucumber Yogurt (page 58), and a
refreshing salad of watermelon, feta, and mint. A nice
combination of hearty and delicate, this meal goes equally
well with beer at a pregame tailgate party or a Domaine
Tempier Bandol Rosé from Provence at a wine country
picnic.

My mom—who is Southern through and through—is a big fan of both salmon and chicken croquettes. I grew up thinking croquettes were distinctly Southern, and I was surprised to spot these little sautéed patties of meat or vegetables on menus in France, Greece, and Italy. For me, there's no better croquette than one made of summer-perfect tomatoes, especially when served with *tzatziki*, a tangy Cucumber Yogurt (page 58). I use plum (Roma) tomatoes, because they're not quite as juicy as other varieties.

Perfect with a chilled white wine, these little patties taste like summer to me. I cooked these at my first James Beard dinner and I couldn't make them fast enough.

Tomato Croquettes with Cucumber Yogurt • DOMATOKEFTETHES ME TZATZIKI

I pound plum (Roma) tomatoes

I cup extra-virgin olive oil, or more as needed

Kosher salt and freshly ground black pepper to taste

$^3/_4$ cup finely chopped yellow onion

2 cloves garlic, minced

I teaspoon finely chopped roasted oil-packed Calabrian chilies (see Resources, page 190) or 2 or 3 small red chilies, roasted

$^1/_2$ cup finely chopped fresh Italian (flat-leaf) parsley

$^1/_2$ cup finely chopped scallions

I teaspoon finely chopped fresh oregano

I teaspoon finely chopped fresh basil

Pinch of sugar, if needed

$^1/_2$ cup all-purpose flour

$^1/_2$ cup dried bread crumbs, preferably panko crumbs (see note, page 122)

Note: Although they aren't used in this dish, the flavored tomato juice and oil can be poured into a plastic bag, sealed, and frozen for use in soups or stews.

Preheat the oven to 350°F.

Core the tomatoes and slice them in half lengthwise. Place in a bowl and toss with $^1/_4$ cup of the olive oil and salt and pepper to taste.

Place the tomatoes on a baking sheet, cut side down. Pour any oil remaining in the bowl over the tomatoes. Bake until the skins are wrinkled and tomatoes are soft, 30 to 40 minutes. Remove from the oven and set aside until cool enough to handle.

Peel the skins from the tomatoes and discard. Place the tomatoes in a colander set over a bowl for about 20 minutes. Press on them occasionally to break them apart and release their juices (see note).

Heat 2 tablespoons of the remaining olive oil in a sauté pan over medium-high heat. Add the onion and sauté until translucent, 3 or 4 minutes. Add the garlic and chilies and stir for another minute. (If you don't have Calabrian chilies, roast, skin, and seed the fresh chilies as directed on page 135.) Pour the onion mixture into a bowl.

Add the drained roasted tomatoes, parsley, scallions, oregano, and basil to the bowl with the onion mixture. Taste the mixture, and if it's at all acidic, add a pinch of sugar. Season with salt and pepper to taste. Mix in the flour and bread crumbs and check again for seasoning.

Divide the mixture into 6 balls and then form into patties about $^1/_2$ inch thick. Heat the remaining 10 tablespoons olive oil in a large skillet. When the oil is hot, add 3 of the patties (the patties should be half-submerged in the oil; add more oil as needed.) Brown for about 3 minutes on the first side, turn, and brown for another 2 to 3 minutes on the second side. Remove and drain on paper towels while cooking the second batch. Sprinkle with salt and eat while warm or let the croquettes cool, place them in a sturdy plastic container, and pack them in your picnic basket.

SERVES **4** TO **6**

If you've got a hungry crowd on your hands, this hearty stuffed sandwich fits the bill. This sandwich is unusual because you dice the lamb sirloin while raw and then cook it in a hot oven inside a hollowed-out loaf of bread. Because the lamb is diced, it cooks much faster than you'd expect. Choose a rustic loaf and don't scoop out too much of the insides when you hollow the loaf; the bread soaks up all the wonderful juices as the lamb cooks with the sautéed onions, garlic, and tomatoes inside the foil wrap.

Cut this into thick slices when you pull the loaf out of the oven, or if you're packing this up for a picnic, keep it wrapped in foil and tightly wrap it in brown paper to hold in the heat until it's time to eat.

You'll find lamb sirloin at the butcher counter of most good markets. If you have trouble finding Myzithra cheese, see Resources on page 190.

You can double or triple this recipe easily, so it's great for Super Bowl parties or any casual get-together. Just fill a two-pound loaf of bread for every four people you're serving. If you're taking this on a wine country picnic for two, make the slices thinner and fan them on a platter before eating. This is a lesson in life as well as in stuffed sandwiches—it's all in how you slice it.

Lamb-and-Cheese-Stuffed Sandwiches •
ARNI KAI MYZITHRA SKOPELOS

One 2-pound loaf of crusty, rustic bread

6 tablespoons extra-virgin olive oil

4 cups minced yellow onions

1 clove garlic, minced

4 plum (Roma) tomatoes, chopped

1 1/2 pounds raw lamb sirloin, cut into 1/2-inch cubes

1/2 teaspoon red pepper flakes

3 teaspoons finely chopped fresh oregano

1 teaspoon finely chopped fresh parsley

1 teaspoon kosher salt

1/4 teaspoon freshly ground black pepper

1 cup grated Myzithra cheese

Preheat the oven to 375°F.

Cut the loaf of bread in half lengthwise and scoop out the soft inner portion of each half, leaving at least 3/4 inch of crust all the way around. Do not leave the crust too thin or tear it.

In a large sauté pan, heat 2 tablespoons of the olive oil over medium-high heat. Add the onions and sauté until translucent, about 3 to 4 minutes. Add the garlic and tomatoes and cook for an additional 3 to 4 minutes. Remove from the heat and set aside to cool.

In a large bowl, toss the diced lamb, red pepper flakes, oregano, parsley, salt, and pepper. Add the tomato mixture and continue tossing until blended.

Brush the inside of the hollowed-out bread loaf with the remaining 4 tablespoons olive oil and sprinkle in the grated cheese. Fill the bottom half of the bread cavity with the meat mixture and carefully place the top half over it, securing it tightly. Wrap tightly with heavy-duty aluminum foil (or double wrap with standard foil), leaving one seam along the top so you can check to see when the meat is cooked. Place the foil-wrapped loaf on a baking sheet and bake for 1 $\frac{1}{2}$ hours. Unwrap the foil at the top seam and check to see if the meat is done. (I like my lamb sirloin cooked until just slightly pink, but cook to your preference.) If the filling isn't piping hot all the way through, rewrap the sandwich in foil and bake for another 20 to 30 minutes.

When done, let the sandwich cool slightly before cutting. Slice and serve warm, or wrap in another layer of foil and pack the sandwich in your picnic basket.

SERVES **4** TO **6**

At first glance, this looks like an odd combination, but luscious, sweet watermelon complements feta's flavor and texture. Lime juice and black pepper bring out the flavors of the fruit and the cheese, and mint ties it all together. When everybody else is bringing watermelon, cantaloupe, and honeydew to the potluck, bring this intriguing mix and see which fruit salad disappears first.

Because the lime juice will macerate the watermelon over time, you'll want to make this salad just before serving. To pack this salad for a picnic, toss together all ingredients except the lime juice. Bring a fresh lime with you, squeeze it over the salad, and toss again just before you sit down to eat.

Watermelon, Feta, and Mint Salad

6 cups diced watermelon (about $^{1}/_{2}$ large watermelon)

1 $^{1}/_{2}$ cups crumbled feta cheese

3 tablespoons finely chopped fresh mint

2 tablespoons fresh lime juice

2 tablespoons extra-virgin olive oil

$^{1}/_{2}$ teaspoon kosher salt

Pinch of freshly ground black pepper

Combine the watermelon, feta, mint, lime juice, and olive oil in a serving bowl and toss gently. Add salt and pepper to taste and toss again. Serve immediately or refrigerate until ready to serve.

SERVES 4 TO 6

MENU

162 • Taki's Cured Sardines with Tomatoes, Olives, and Bread (SARDELES TAKIS)

165 • Skillet Leek Pizza (TIGANOPITA ME PRASO)

167 • Baked Eggplant with Meat and Béchamel Sauce (MOUSSAKA)

169 • Custard-Filled Phyllo Triangles (BOUGATSA)

SIPPING SPIRITS WITH GREEK MEZES · Set out mezes, or small plates, and bring out the ouzo

I first learned to salt-cure fresh fish by watching my godfather, Peter J. Costas (called "Taki" by my family) make these sardines. In the Greek Orthodox Church, a godparent literally becomes part of the family, and it was a tradition in our house to cook big meals with Taki and his wife, Maria.

I was a teenager when Taki showed me how he lifted the bones from a sardine fillet. He said, "Here, you can do this," and when I did it, I was so pleased to master the task. I feel very lucky to have Taki in my life, passing along to me the cooking traditions that were passed along to him by his grandfather. You, too, can debone and salt-cure a fresh sardine. It's not hard, and the flavor of these sardines makes it worth the effort. If you're like me, you'll find enormous satisfaction in placing your own cured sardines on the table with tomatoes, good olives, and a crusty loaf of bread.

Skillet Pizza sounds like a heavy meal, but is actually much lighter than a standard pizza pie. Closer to Italian focaccia bread than pizza in spirit, with an airy pizza "crust" that's light and yet very crisp on the bottom, my skillet pizza is topped simply with fresh leek slices, feta cheese, and freshly ground black pepper. A slice of this goes very well with your own salt-cured sardines and a wedge of moussaka.

Moussaka has gotten a bad rap. This lasagna-like dish uses sliced eggplant instead of pasta, layered with a hearty meat sauce and a nutmeg-flavored béchamel sauce. Serve moussaka beside a standard lasagna, and watch as your guests sample both. I bet at least once during the meal you hear somebody say, "I've never liked eggplant but this is really good." Whenever I hear this, I think, "Yes! One more moussaka convert!" The trick is to lightly salt your eggplant slices, allow the salt to pull out some of the bitterness, and then rinse each slice in cool running water. I've included detailed instructions in the recipe.

Bougatsa is a finger-food dessert that I serve at parties all year long. Flavored with orange zest and Cointreau, the soft, smooth custard center is surrounded by lots of flaky pastry, folded into a triangle the way you'd fold a flag. Even in Greece, these triangles are not as well known as baklava or the *galatoboureko* (page 38), but I think they're addictive.

Few Americans get to taste fresh sardines, deboned and cured briefly in sea salt, lemon juice, and fresh oregano. This is a pity, because served with bread, olives, and fresh tomatoes, these sardines are just about the best appetizer I can think of.

As with any fish, sardines need to be as fresh as can be. Look for fish that are bright and shiny, and walk away from any sardine that appears dull. See "Buying Fresh Fish" on page 88.

If your sardines are bigger than 8 to 10 fish per pound, follow these same steps but cut each fish in half or thirds to fit the size of your tomato slice.

Gray sea salt has a lovely flavor, but if you've never cooked with this damp salt, you may be at a loss when you open the container. Just spread the salt onto a baking sheet and either place it in a sunny spot for a day or two or warm it in your oven under very low heat for a few hours. If your salt grinder has metal blades, don't store sea salt inside the grinder because its blades will corrode. If you have a mortar and pestle, use this to grind your dried salt. If you don't, place the dried salt in a resealable plastic bag, and crush the salt with a heavy rolling pin. See Resources, page 190, for sea salt and a sea salt grinder.

Taki's Cured Sardines with Tomatoes, Olives, and Bread • SARDELES TAKIS

2 pounds small, fresh sardines

1 pound dried and ground gray sea salt

1/4 cup fresh lemon juice

1/4 cup extra-virgin olive oil

1 tablespoon finely chopped fresh oregano

4 tomatoes

20 Kalamata olives, pitted

1 small loaf crusty, rustic bread

Clean the sardines by cutting the heads and tails off with scissors. Pull out the viscera and rinse the cavities under cold running water. Lay the cleaned sardines on paper towels to drain and dry. With the end of a sharp knife, lift the tail end of the bony spine of 1 sardine and gently pull the spine away from the flesh. It should lift out easily. (If not, gently prod the flesh near the spine with the tip of the knife to loosen it from the soft bone.) If the butterfly fold of the fish does not stay intact after removing the backbone, simply place the sardine halves together as if the fish were whole. Lay it in a 9-by-13-inch baking dish. Repeat with the remaining sardines.

When all the sardines are cleaned and boned, coat the insides of each fish with a covering of dry, crushed gray salt and close the fillet. Coat the outsides with more gray salt and place back in the dish, drying the dish out if necessary. Cover securely with plastic wrap or aluminum foil and place in the refrigerator for at least 12 hours.

When ready to use, rinse the sardines thoroughly with cold water, pat dry, and slice in half to separate the fillets.

In a small bowl, whisk the lemon juice, olive oil, and oregano together. Slice the tomatoes to fit the size of the sardine pieces and arrange on a large platter. Place a sardine fillet on each tomato slice. Pour the lemon and olive oil dressing over the fish. Toss the olives randomly over the top, and serve with thick slices of the bread for a meze.

SERVES 10 TO 12

Forget about the tomato sauce and mozzarella. My Greek-style pizza has the simple toppings of a foccacia on a yeast-based dough round that's browned in a skillet to make the bottom extra crisp and then puffed in the oven.

This recipe makes enough dough for six medium pizzas. If you want to make the dough ahead of time, cover it tightly with plastic wrap and store in your refrigerator. Pull the dough from the fridge twenty minutes before rolling so it has a chance to warm up a little.

You can also freeze half of this dough for as long as a month or two (although the longer it's frozen, the less I like its flavor). Be sure to let the dough thaw completely before you work with it.

Skillet Leek Pizza • TIGANOPITA ME PRASO

$1/_4$ cup warm water (105°F)

1 $1/_8$ teaspoons dry yeast ($1/_2$ envelope)

$1/_2$ cup room temperature water

3 tablespoons extra-virgin olive oil, plus extra for greasing

2 cups all-purpose flour, plus extra for dusting

1 $1/_2$ teaspoons kosher salt, plus extra for garnish

$1/_2$ cup thinly sliced, cleaned leeks

6 tablespoons olive oil

I cup crumbled feta cheese

Freshly ground black pepper

Put the warm water in a small bowl and sprinkle the yeast on top. Let stand until the yeast softens, 3 to 5 minutes. Mix slightly to dissolve the yeast and let it proof for another 15 minutes in a warm spot in the kitchen. Add the room temperature water and 1 tablespoon of the extra-virgin olive oil to the yeast mixture and stir to combine. Combine the flour and 1 teaspoon of the salt in the bowl of a stand mixer fitted with the paddle attachment and mix on very low speed. Slowly add the liquid ingredients to the dry and increase the speed of the mixer slightly to incorporate the mass. Stop the mixer and replace the paddle with a dough hook if you have one. Knead until the dough becomes smooth and begins to pull away from the sides of the bowl, about 4 minutes. Place the dough on a lightly floured board and knead the dough by hand for another minute or two. Dust with flour as needed to prevent sticking. Shape the dough into a ball and place in a very lightly oiled bowl and cover with a clean kitchen towel. Let stand until dough doubles in bulk, about 1 hour.

Heat the remaining 2 tablespoons extra-virgin olive oil in a sauté pan over medium heat. Add the leeks. Raise the heat to medium-high and sweat the leeks with the remaining $1/_2$ teaspoon salt until soft and translucent, about 3 to 4 minutes. Reduce the heat if the leeks begin to brown. Set aside and let cool.

Preheat the oven to 350°F.

When the dough has doubled in bulk, divide it into 6 equal pieces (about 6 ounces each). Set the pieces of dough being used on a baking sheet and cover with a clean kitchen towel or plastic wrap. (Dough not being used can be placed in the refrigerator or frozen until ready to use.) With a rolling pin on a lightly floured surface, roll each piece of dough as evenly as possible into a 6-inch circle, dusting lightly with flour as needed.

continued

Heat 1 tablespoon of the olive oil in a large skillet. Place one dough round in the hot skillet and allow it to brown and puff for 1 to 2 minutes. With tongs or a metal spatula, flip the pizza over and brown briefly on the other side. Once browned, remove the pizza from the pan and place on an ovenproof platter. Sprinkle the top with 2 $\frac{1}{2}$ tablespoons of the feta, a generous tablespoon of the sautéed leeks, a quick grind of pepper, and a pinch of salt. Repeat for each pizza. Place all the pizzas in the oven and bake just long enough for the cheese to melt.

Pull from the oven, cut each into 6 pieces, and serve immediately.

SERVES **4** TO **6** AS A MAIN COURSE,
OR **10** TO **12** AS AN APPETIZER OR SMALL PLATE

3 medium purple eggplants

2 teaspoons kosher salt

$^1/_2$ cup olive oil, or as needed

Meat Sauce

2 tablespoons unsalted butter

2 yellow onions, finely chopped

$^3/_4$ pound ground beef

$^1/_2$ cup dry white wine

2 tablespoons tomato paste

$^1/_2$ cup water

2 tablespoons chopped fresh Italian (flat-leaf) parsley

$^1/_2$ teaspoon ground cinnamon

$^1/_2$ teaspoon kosher salt

$^1/_4$ teaspoon freshly ground black pepper

Béchamel Sauce

4 tablespoons unsalted butter

4 tablespoons all-purpose flour

2 cups whole milk

$^1/_2$ teaspoon freshly grated nutmeg

2 teaspoons kosher salt

Freshly ground black pepper to taste

1 cup grated Kefalotyri cheese (see Resources, page 190), plus 1 cup for assembly

Butter for greasing

Note: Eggplant acts as a sponge when it come in contact with oil, so keep the oil to a minimum and make sure it is hot and evenly distributed in the pan. Salting the eggplant before sautéing also helps the eggplant absorb less oil.

Moussaka is one of those classic Greek country dishes that calls for lots of vegetables (here, roasted eggplant with a nutmeg-flavored béchamel sauce) to stretch out a little meat. Perfect for any guests trying to avoid carbs, this protein-packed layered dish uses sliced eggplant instead of pasta.

My mom made moussaka all the time when I was a girl, and it was one of my least favorite meals. My brothers, Mike and Chris, and I would groan when she brought out the baking dish filled with steaming eggplant and meat sauce layered with béchamel. My mom and dad both loved it, so she just kept making it and ignoring her children. Good thing, too. It's a mystery to me how a food you disliked as a child can become an adult favorite, but that's how it is with moussaka. These days, I see a good moussaka, and my mouth begins to water.

Baked Eggplant with Meat and Béchamel Sauce • MOUSSAKA

Wash the eggplants and cut off the ends. With a small paring knife, working with one eggplant at a time, peel $^1/_2$-inch strips of the skin from the stem down, making stripes around the eggplant. Place it on its side and carefully slice crosswise into even, $^1/_3$-inch-thick rounds. Repeat with the remaining eggplants. Sparingly, use the 2 teaspoons salt to very lightly sprinkle both sides of all the slices, spreading the salt with your fingers. Don't use more than 2 teaspoons of salt—a little salt goes a long way. Place the salted slices on a large flat tray lined with paper towels. Layer them between additional towels if necessary and let sit for approximately 30 minutes. Rinse the slices well under cold running water and immediately pat dry and set aside.

In a very large sauté pan, heat 2 tablespoons of the olive oil over medium-high heat. Make sure the oil is hot and evenly distributed over the surface of the pan. Carefully add 6 to 8 eggplant slices (or as many as the pan will fit comfortably), one at a time, and fry, turning once, until the eggplant is golden brown on both sides, about 3 to 4 minutes per side. Using tongs, remove the eggplant from the pan and place on a tray lined with paper towels. Continue frying the remaining eggplant in batches, repeating the process with 2 tablespoons of oil each time until all the eggplant has been browned, drained, and cooled (see note).

To make the meat sauce, in a large skillet, melt the butter over medium heat, being careful not to brown it. Add the chopped onions and cook until tender and translucent, 3 to 4 minutes. Add the ground beef and brown for about 6 minutes. Add the wine and scrape the bottom of the pan with a spatula or spoon to deglaze, loosening any browned bits stuck on the bottom. Bring to a simmer and cook to reduce the

continued

liquid until the pan is almost dry. Add the tomato paste, water, parsley, cinnamon, salt, and pepper and let the mixture cook over very low heat for about 20 minutes. The sauce should be moist and spreadable but it will have much less liquid than a standard pasta sauce. Remove from the heat and let cool.

To make the béchamel sauce, in a saucepan, melt the butter over medium-high heat. Blend in the flour with a whisk and cook until bubbly but not brown, 2 to 3 minutes. Gradually pour in the milk, whisking it into the butter-and-flour roux thoroughly until the mixture is thick and smooth. Remove the mixture from the heat and add the nutmeg, salt, and pepper to taste and blend thoroughly. Let the mixture cool slightly, then add I cup of the grated cheese, stirring until blended.

Preheat the oven to 350°F.

Before assembling the moussaka, butter a 9-by-13-by-2-inch baking dish. Arrange half of the eggplant on the bottom of the pan and spread half of the meat mixture over it. Repeat with another layer of eggplant and top with the remaining meat mixture. Spread the béchamel sauce evenly over the meat mixture, and then sprinkle the remaining I cup cheese over the top. Bake for 40 minutes or until casserole is piping hot and the cheese has melted and browned slightly. Transfer to a wire rack and let cool for about 20 minutes. Cut into 3-inch squares and serve warm.

SERVES 12

Orange zest, orange liqueur, and cinnamon flavor the custard filling in my *bougatsa*. If you put out a big platter of these treats at a party, keep on eye on them. It's fun to watch people taste them and then keep coming back for more. These addictive little triangles are a terrific finger food for both summer- and winter-time parties.

See "Tips for Handling Phyllo Dough" on page 39 before you begin this recipe.

Custard-Filled Phyllo Triangles •
BOUGATSA

12 sheets phyllo dough

2 large eggs

$^1/_2$ cup granulated sugar

2 cups whole milk

$^1/_3$ cup semolina flour

1 teaspoon vanilla extract

1 teaspoon grated orange zest (see page 22)

2 tablespoons Cointreau or other orange liqueur

$^1/_2$ cup unsalted butter, melted

$^3/_4$ cup confectioners' sugar

1 teaspoon ground cinnamon

1 cup finely ground walnuts or pecans

Preheat the oven to 350°F.

Remove the phyllo dough from the refrigerator. Keep tightly wrapped and let come to room temperature while preparing the filling.

Beat the eggs with an electric mixer on high speed until light in color. Add the granulated sugar and continue to beat until the mixture is thick and fluffy. In a saucepan, bring the milk to a simmer over medium heat. Reduce the heat to keep the milk at a steady simmer (be careful not to let it scald) and slowly add the semolina, stirring all the while. Continue to stir and cook the mixture over low heat until thickened. Remove from the heat. Place 2 tablespoons of the hot semolina into the egg mixture to temper (see note, page 79), beating thoroughly. Transfer the egg, sugar, and semolina mixture from the bowl into the saucepan, thoroughly combining with the remaining semolina and milk. Place the saucepan over very low heat, stirring constantly until the mixture is smooth and thick. Remove from the heat. Add the vanilla, orange zest, and orange liqueur and mix thoroughly. Set aside and let cool.

In a small saucepan, melt the butter over very low heat. Unfold the package of phyllo and separate 12 sheets from the stack. (Place the remainder of the dough back into the package and refrigerate for another use.) Set the phyllo sheets on a flat work surface and cover with a clean, lightly dampened kitchen towel.

Remove 1 sheet, lay it flat, and brush completely with butter. Fold the dough lengthwise into thirds to make a rectangle about 4 inches by 12 inches. Spoon 2 heaping tablespoons of the semolina custard onto the inside lower left corner of the rectangle, about 2 inches above the edge. Begin with the lower right edge and fold it over the mound of custard to form a triangle. Continue folding, end to end, as if folding a flag into a triangle, until the entire piece of dough has been folded. Brush the folded triangle lightly with butter and place on a baking sheet. Repeat until all the phyllo and custard have been used.

Bake until the triangles are golden brown, 15 to 20 minutes. Remove from the oven. Sift confectioners' sugar and cinnamon over the tops of the warm triangles and sprinkle with finely ground walnuts or pecans. Serve warm.

SERVES 12

MENU

173 • Grilled Artichokes with Caper Aioli
(AGGINARES SKARAS KAPPORI SALTSA)

174 • Grilled Prawns with Egg and
Lemon Froth (GARIDES TIS SKARAS AVGOLEMONO)

176 • Grilled Lamb Chops
with Alma's Fruited Mustard
(ARNI TIS SKARAS ME MOUSTARTHA)

178 • Skopelos-Style Grilled Potatoes
(PATATES ME LEMONE)

181 • Grilled Stonefruit with Prosciutto
and Sheep's Cheese (VEIKOKO SKIN SKARAS ME TIRI)

FIRING UP MY FAMOUS ALL-GRILL SUPPER • Friends help carry my dining table into the backyard

Cooking an entire dinner on the grill is Greek in spirit but definitely Californian in style. I first cooked an all-grill dinner at home because I couldn't bear to cook indoors on a perfect Indian summer evening. I made my friends help me drag the dining room table outside next to the grill, and while I cooked I got to join in the conversation and feel the last of the summer breezes. I thought about my relatives in Skopelos and eating at their enormous table under the trees while Uncle Yiorgios cooked a whole goat over a fire pit, and it occurred to me that dining and cooking outdoors may just be in my blood.

The star of this show is the lamb. I like lamb chops cut from the loin *scottadito*-style. In Italian, this means "burn your fingers"—you have no choice but to pick up these delicate little chops by the bone. Greeks cut lamb very differently. For special occasions (which happen fairly often) Greeks cook the lamb whole over a pit, and when the meat comes off the fire, they follow the "use a big knife, get it on the table fast" rule of carving. These grilled chops have more finesse (and take much less of a toll on the cook), but the Greek way of grilling a whole lamb and carving just before serving tasted better than any lamb I've tried.

Grilling whole artichokes or fruit may be new to you, but you'll be surprised by how easy it is, and how much the fire enhances their taste. Every dish on this menu gains an extra layer of flavor from cooking over a fire. The fruit and vegetables in particular look so good that a beautiful presentation just means arranging them on a platter.

I'm a fan of artichoke hearts, but I like this cooking method better because nothing is wasted. When I first became a chef and saw the mountains of leaves tossed away while we cooked the artichoke hearts, I couldn't help but think of my mom and how she'd hate to see all those leaves go uneaten. With this recipe, not a bit of the artichoke is wasted.

The smoky taste of the grill suits the rich, dense flavor of the artichokes, and the creamy dipping sauce, similar to a New Orleans–style rémoulade, gets an extra flavor kick from capers or sauce, Calabrian chilies, garlic, and lemon juice. I like my aioli spicy; you may want to add 1 teaspoon of the Calabrian chilies, taste the aioli, and see if you'd like more heat.

If you like, make the aioli the day before, cover and refrigerate, and bring it to the table when the artichokes are done.

Grilled Artichokes with Caper Aioli •
AGGINARES SKARAS KAPPORI SALTSA

Aioli

2 egg yolks

I clove garlic, minced

2 teaspoons fresh lemon juice

2 $^{1}/_{4}$ cups light olive oil

I tablespoon chopped roasted oil-packed Calabrian chilies (see Resources, page 190) or 2 or 3 red chilies

I teaspoon capers, drained

I teaspoon kosher salt

$^{1}/_{2}$ teaspoon freshly ground black pepper

2 tablespoons kosher salt, plus 2 teaspoons

I lemon, halved, plus 3 tablespoons fresh lemon juice

3 large artichokes, $^{1}/_{2}$ inch of woody stem trimmed, but the rest remaining

6 tablespoons extra-virgin olive oil

$^{1}/_{2}$ teaspoon freshly ground black pepper

Prepare a fire in a charcoal grill or preheat a gas grill.

To make the aioli, combine the egg yolks, garlic, and lemon juice in a blender or food processor. Process at medium-high speed to blend, then very slowly add the oil in a thin stream through the pouring tube while the machine is running. When the mixture has thickened, turn off the machine, add the chilies, capers, salt, and pepper, and pulse until well mixed. (If you don't have Calabrian chilies, roast, skin, and seed the fresh peppers as directed on page 135.) If the aioli is too thick, add a little water. Refrigerate while the artichokes are grilling.

Fill a stockpot halfway with water and add the 2 tablespoons salt and the lemon halves. Bring to a boil. Add the artichokes, cover, and cook for 35 minutes. When ready, a large leaf should come off easily when gently pulled. Drain and let cool.

Cut the artichokes in half lengthwise and scoop out the center choke (the fuzzy section and the purple leaves). Rub I tablespoon olive oil and $^{1}/_{2}$ tablespoon lemon juice on each cut side of the halved artichokes. Sprinkle all with the 2 teaspoons salt and the pepper. Place the artichokes on the grill, cut side down, and grill for 5 to 6 minutes. Flip and grill for I minute longer.

To serve, place the artichokes on individual plates. Spoon the aioli into small ramekins and give an individual serving to each guest, or set one big bowl of aioli on the table and let everybody dip in.

SERVES 4 TO 6

We're cheating a little on our all-grill menu here, because this dish is partly cooked in the oven, but it requires little kitchen time, so you'll still be able to spend time outside with your guests.

Avgolemono is the classic Greek mixture of egg and lemon. We typically think of it as soup, but I love it as a thick, lemony sauce over seafood, and with grilled prawns it's especially good. The only trick with *avgolemono* is to temper the egg-lemon mixture by ladling in a little of the hot liquid while you whisk. That way, the egg doesn't cook or harden, but stays creamy when you pour it over the prawns and cook it in the oven. I like this dish spicy; for a milder version, cut the amount of red pepper flakes in half.

Grilled Prawns with Egg and Lemon Froth • GARIDES TIS SKARAS AVGOLEMONO

6 wooden skewers, soaked in warm water for 1 hour

1/4 cup extra-virgin olive oil

1 tablespoon finely chopped fresh oregano

3 cloves garlic, minced

1 teaspoon red pepper flakes

2 teaspoons kosher salt

1 teaspoon freshly ground black pepper

24 prawns or large shrimp, clean and deveined, tails intact

1/2 cup fish stock or bottled clam broth

1/2 cup finely chopped tomatoes

1 large egg

1/4 cup fresh lemon juice

1 1/2 teaspoons finely chopped fresh Italian (flat-leaf) parsley

Preheat the oven to 450°F. Prepare a fire in a charcoal grill or preheat a gas grill.

While the wooden skewers are soaking, stir together the olive oil, oregano, garlic, red pepper flakes, salt, and pepper in large bowl. Add the prawns and marinate in the refrigerator for at least 1 hour.

Slide 4 prawns onto each skewer. Place on the hot grill and mark on both sides quickly, for about 1 minute on each side, not cooking them through. Put them in a baking dish and pour the fish stock over the prawns. Add the chopped tomatoes and place the dish in the oven for approximately 4 minutes.

Pull the dish from the oven, take the prawns out of the stock, and place them on a shallow, warmed platter. In a bowl, whisk together the egg and lemon juice. Temper the egg mixture by ladling a small amount of the hot fish stock in while you whisk vigorously (see note, page 79). Slowly pour in the rest of the fish stock from the baking dish until incorporated and foamy. Pour the sauce over the prawns and sprinkle with the parsley. Serve warm as an appetizer.

SERVES 4 TO 6

Alma Brothers, my mother's mother, was famous on Swan Lake in Jackson, Mississippi, for her spicy, sweet mustard. She'd make a big batch every Christmas, and people in the town would call and beg to be on her holiday list. When I was a girl, I thought her mustard was way too strong—but Alma didn't make it with children in mind. Now that my tastes are more sophisticated, I love this sweet-hot blend. Its flavor has more clarity than the store-bought mustards you're accustomed to. I used her recipe as the base for my fruited mustard, making it richer with rosemary browned butter and fresher tasting with the addition of tart, dried cherries. My mom and I bring out Alma's mustard every holiday, which makes me feel at every gathering that Alma's spirit carries on.

Grilled Lamb Chops with Alma's Fruited Mustard • ARNI TIS SKARAS ME MOUSTARTHA

Fruited Mustard

2 pounds (8 sticks) unsalted butter

2 bay leaves, chopped

1 tablespoon chopped fresh rosemary

1 cup chopped dried cherries

Freshly ground black pepper to taste

1 cup Alma's Sweet-Hot Mustard (page 187)

2 cups Dijon mustard

4 loin lamb chops, each about 1 inch thick

Extra-virgin olive oil for brushing

Kosher salt and freshly ground black pepper to taste

Prepare a fire in a charcoal grill or preheat a gas grill.

To make the fruited mustard, in a saucepan, melt the butter over medium heat and cook until it reaches a caramel color, 3 to 4 minutes. Add the bay leaves, rosemary, dried cherries, and pepper. Mix in the sweet and Dijon mustards. Refrigerate while the lamb chops are grilling.

Brush each of the chops on both sides with olive oil and season with salt and pepper. Grill for 4 to 5 minutes on each side for medium-rare lamb.

Serve immediately with the fruited mustard either beside the lamb or spooned into small ramekins and set on a plate garnished with dried cherries and herbs. (Make sandwiches the next day with any leftover lamb plus a generous slathering of the mustard.)

SERVES **4**

My favorite potatoes, I discovered these in the tavernas on Skopelos. There, they boil plain russet potatoes, cut them in half, slather them with olive oil and a little butter, douse them with lemon juice, and sprinkle on some sea salt and freshly ground pepper. Then they're placed on the grill, cut side down, where they form a delicious, lemony crust. Just thinking about them makes my mouth water. In the summer, I use the same technique with corn, rubbing the husked ears with olive oil and butter, and then squeezing on some fresh lime juice and maybe sprinkling a little chili powder.

You can add herbs or not to these potatoes. I grill these all summer long and like to use a different combination of herbs each time.

Skopelos-Style Grilled Potatoes ◆
PATATES ME LEMONE

2 large russet potatoes, unpeeled (about 1 ³/₄ pounds total)

¹/₄ cup extra-virgin olive oil

2 tablespoons fresh lemon juice

1 teaspoon kosher salt

¹/₂ teaspoon freshly ground black pepper

1 tablespoon chopped mixed fresh herbs such as rosemary and thyme (optional)

Put the potatoes in a 4-quart pot with salted water and bring to a boil. Boil for about 30 minutes, or until fork tender.

Prepare a fire in a charcoal grill or preheat a gas grill.

Cut the potatoes in half lengthwise and arrange the potato halves, cut side up, on a plate.

In a bowl, whisk together the olive oil, lemon juice, salt, pepper, and herbs, if using. Pour over the potatoes and let sit for 10 minutes.

Cook the potatoes on the hot grill, cut side down, until crisp outside and tender when pierced with a knife, 5 to 6 minutes. Serve hot.

SERVES **4**

You have to try this dessert, which combines lush, ripe summer fruit, cured meat, and a melting slice of rich cheese. It's sweet and salty, silky and satiny, a whole range of textures in one bite.

Cutting the fruit in half and grilling it lightly brings out all its flavor. When you layer on the prosciutto, drape it in such a way that you can see a glimpse of fruit on either side of the meat.

You need perfect fruit for this recipe. If the fruit near you isn't impeccable, see Resources on page 190 for truly amazing apricots, nectarines, plums, and pluots, all of which work beautifully for this recipe.

Grilled Stonefruit with Prosciutto and Sheep's Cheese ◆
VEIKOKO SKIN SKARAS ME TIRI

8 ripe but firm apricots, halved and pitted

Extra-virgin olive oil for brushing and drizzling

Kosher salt and freshly ground black pepper to taste

8 paper-thin slices prosciutto, cut in half crosswise

$^1/_2$ cup kasseri cheese or other sheep's cheese shavings (see note, page 145)

Prepare a fire in a charcoal grill or preheat a gas grill on high.

Brush each apricot half with olive oil and sprinkle with salt and pepper. Place on a hot area of the grill for 1 minute on each side, to lightly grill-mark the apricots. Remove from the grill when they're just warm and place on a warmed platter. Drape the prosciutto lightly over the apricots so you can see a bit of the fruit. Lay the pieces of cheese over the prosciutto. Lightly drizzle olive oil over the fruit, cheese, and prosciutto and serve immediately.

SERVES **4** TO **6**

184 ◆ Roasted Chicken Stock

185 ◆ Roasted Veal Stock

186 ◆ Pickled Mushrooms
(MANITARIA TURSI)

187 ◆ Alma's Sweet-Hot Mustard

188 ◆ Preserved Lemons

189 ◆ Basil Oil

THE PANTRY

Greek country cooking is like Italian cooking, in that a well-stocked pantry is the heart of every kitchen. These recipes are the basics of my cooking. If you came to my home you'd find every one of these in either my pantry or my freezer.

Some recipes, like the roasted chicken stock, were refined over years of cooking in restaurant kitchens. Other recipes, like my grandmother Alma's mustard-with-a-kick, are cherished family recipes.

These staples are called for in many recipes in this book, but you can use them to add extra flavor to your own recipes as well.

Roasting the chicken bones before you make a stock gives it a heartier flavor and rich color. This is the single recipe I use most often; I always, always have pints of this stacked neatly in my freezer.

Roasted Chicken Stock

Preheat the oven to 450°F.

Rinse the chicken bones to remove excess blood. Place the chicken bones in a flameproof roasting pan large enough to hold the bones in one layer without over-crowding them. If the bones are very lean, toss them with a light coating of olive oil to help them brown. Place in the oven and brown, stirring occasionally. The finished bones should be richly caramelized and brown. This could take 45 minutes or as long as 1 hour.

5 pounds chicken bones, preferably backs

Extra-virgin olive oil, if needed

1 large yellow onion, cut into 1-inch pieces

2 large carrots, cut into 1-inch pieces

2 celery stalks, cut into 1-inch pieces

10 to 12 cups cold water

2 bay leaves

12 peppercorns

1 cup dry red wine

Remove the bones from the pan and place them in a stockpot. Add the vegetables to the roasting pan. If there is fat from the chicken bones, toss the vegetables in it to coat them lightly. If not, toss the vegetables with a light coating of olive oil. Return the pan to the oven to brown the vegetables, about 20 to 30 minutes.

Meanwhile, pour enough of the cold water over the bones to cover them completely. Bring to a boil over high heat, skimming any foam that rises to the top. Reduce the heat to low and simmer gently for about 30 minutes.

Add the browned vegetables to the stockpot along with the bay leaves and pepper-corns. Place the roasting pan over a burner, add the wine to the pan, and bring to a simmer. Scrape the bottom of the pan with a spoon or spatula to deglaze, loosening any browned bits. Cook to reduce to about $1/2$ cup. Add to the stockpot.

Simmer the stock for 6 hours, skimming off any fat or impurities that rise to the surface. If the level of liquid reduces below the top of the bones, add more water to the pot. Drain the finished stock through a fine-mesh strainer and discard the bones and vegetables.

You should have about 2 quarts of liquid. If you have more, reheat the stock in a pot and simmer until it has reduced to 2 quarts. Cool the stock to room temperature, then pour into one or several locktop plastic containers. Once the stock has chilled, the fat will rise to the top and solidify. Lift it off and discard. The stock can be refrig-erated for up to 2 weeks or frozen for longer storage.

MAKES **2 QUARTS**

When beef stock is called for, this is the stock I used. As with the chicken stock, this sits in my freezer at all times, stacked in pint containers.

Roasted Veal Stock

Preheat the oven to 450°F.

Place the veal bones in a roasting pan large enough to hold the bones in one layer without overcrowding them. If the bones are very lean, toss them with a light coating of olive oil to help them brown. Place in the oven and brown, stirring occasionally. The finished bones should be richly caramelized and brown. This could take 45 minutes or as long as 1 hour.

Remove the bones from the pan and place them in a stockpot. Add the vegetables to the roasting pan. If there is fat from the veal bones, toss the vegetables in it to coat them lightly. If not, toss the vegetables with a light coating of olive oil. Return the pan to the oven to brown the vegetables, 20 to 30 minutes.

5 pounds meaty veal bones

Extra-virgin olive oil, if needed

1 large yellow onion, cut into 1-inch pieces

2 large carrots, cut into 1-inch pieces

2 celery stalks, cut into 1-inch pieces

10 to 12 cups cold water

2 bay leaves

12 peppercorns

1 cup dry red wine

Meanwhile, pour enough of the cold water over the bones to cover them completely. Bring to a boil over high heat, skimming any foam that rises to the top. Reduce the heat to low and simmer gently for about 30 minutes.

Add the browned vegetables to the stockpot along with the bay leaves and peppercorns. Place the roasting pan over a burner, add the wine to the pan and bring to a simmer. Scrape the bottom of the pan with a spoon or spatula to deglaze, loosening any browned bits. Cook to reduce to about $1/2$ cup. Add to the stockpot.

Simmer the stock for 6 hours, skimming off any fat or impurities that rise to the surface. If the level of liquid reduces below the top of the bones, add more water to the pot. Drain the finished stock through a fine-mesh strainer and discard the bones and vegetables.

You should have about 2 quarts of liquid. If you have more, reheat the stock in a pot and simmer until it has reduced to 2 quarts. Cool the stock to room temperature, then pour into one or several locktop plastic containers. Once the stock has chilled, the fat will rise to the top and solidify. Lift it off and discard. The stock can be refrigerated for up to 2 weeks or frozen for longer storage.

MAKES **2** QUARTS

In the Aegean Islands in Greece, mountain villagers go on mushroom hunts, with entire families scouting the hillsides for perfect mushrooms. Of all the mushroom dishes I tasted in Greece, the pickled mushrooms had the most distinctive, intriguing flavor.

You can use any type of mushroom for this recipe, but I find that bite-sized mushrooms pickle best. Keep in mind that mushrooms soak up water like little sponges. Rather than washing them in water to clean them, just brush them clean with a small, soft brush. Trim off any part of the stem that you wouldn't relish eating.

Pickled Mushrooms • MANITARIA TURSI

I tablespoon plus 1 ½ teaspoons kosher salt

2 tablespoons fresh lemon juice

I pound fresh whole porcini, shiitake, or cremini mushrooms, brushed clean

⅓ cup extra-virgin olive oil

I cup champagne or white wine vinegar

6 peppercorns

I dried chile, preferably arbol (see note)

I tablespoon fresh savory

I tablespoon fresh oregano

2 bay leaves

Note: The arbol is my favorite chile to use when cooking Mexican foods, and it adds just the right spice to these mushrooms. This long chile may be thin but it packs a lot of heat! Don't toss in more than one unless you're very experienced with hot chilies.

In a stockpot, bring 2 quarts of water to a boil. Add the salt, lemon juice, and mushrooms. Let the mushrooms blanch for 4 to 5 minutes. Drain the mushrooms in a colander. Pat the mushrooms dry with a clean kitchen towel or paper towel and place in a glass jar or a heavy plastic container. (I prefer glass, but either way your container must have a tight-fitting lid.)

In a stainless-steel saucepan, thoroughly heat the olive oil with the vinegar, peppercorns, chile, savory, oregano, and bay leaves. Pour the hot mixture over the mushrooms and let them sit at room temperature for 20 minutes. Put the lid on the container when the mixture has cooled, then place in the refrigerator to chill and marinate for at least 48 hours before serving.

When the mushrooms are refrigerated, the oil and vinegar separates and the oil comes to the top and solidifies. Allow the mixture to come to room temperature before serving so the liquids can mingle.

MAKES I PINT

How do you transform simple ham and bread into a satisfying lunch? My Alma's Sweet-Hot Mustard does the trick. I serve this with lamb (page 176) and mix it with bourbon to glaze pork (page 27), but I think its pure, bright flavor is heaven just pulled out of the fridge and slathered on a sandwich.

My grandmother's mustard has always been famous with the people who knew and loved her. One of the best things about this mustard—besides how exceptionally delicious it is—is that it can be made ahead and in big batches because it keeps for a good period of time. When the holidays roll around, it makes a perfect gift for friends. (Be forewarned: Once you give someone a jar of this mustard, they will hound you for more jars forever after.) Because I was so close to my grandmother, I cherish her recipe and hope to hand it down to my kids and grandkids. This is the best kind of family legacy, because those of us who knew and loved Alma get to remember her every time we taste her mustard.

I often stir a tablespoon of fruit into this mustard just before serving. I especially like dried cherries (rehydrate them in warm water for a few minutes, then drain off the water), but dried apricots and fresh diced apples work well, too.

$1/2$ cup dry Coleman's mustard (one 2-ounce can)

$1/2$ cup sugar

$1/2$ teaspoon kosher salt

1 tablespoon all-purpose flour

$1/2$ cup apple cider vinegar

1 tablespoon unsalted butter, melted

1 cup plus 2 tablespoons prepared yellow mustard (9 ounces)

Alma's Sweet-Hot Mustard

Mix together the dry mustard, sugar, salt, and flour. Stir the vinegar and melted butter into the dry mustard mixture, then add the prepared mustard. Blend well. Refrigerate the mustard for at least 24 hours to allow the mustard powder to come to its full heat and meld with the rest of the ingredients.

MAKES ABOUT 1 $1/2$ CUPS

Intensely flavorful, these preserved lemons are a definitive ingredient in many Greek dishes, as well as many Middle Eastern cuisines. They're the perfect addition to spark up fresh spinach leaves (page 71), or chop a few spoonfuls of these and toss over salads or vegetables.

These lemons rest for at least two weeks after you cut, salt, and immerse them in juice. There's a trick to how you should cut these lemons; you want them quartered but intact. Make a cut straight down from pole to pole without cutting through the bottom of the lemon. Then, on the same side, make another cut perpendicular to your first cut, again without cutting through the bottom. The lemon will resemble a flower. This cut allows you to pack the lemons amply with salt, to better preserve them.

Preserved Lemons

10 lemons

5 to 6 cups kosher salt (about 2 pounds)

2 cups fresh lemon juice

2 $\frac{1}{2}$ to 3 cups water

4 bay leaves

15 peppercorns

Choose a container with a tight-fitting lid, such as a large Ball jar or Tupperware container. (I prefer glass just because I like to see the lemons through the glass.)

Quarter the lemons without cutting all the way through the bottom. Place the lemons on a sheet of parchment paper. Fill each cut lemon with about 3 tablespoons of salt—or as much salt as you can—keeping the lemon in one piece and taking care not to break it. Gently push the lemon back together as if the lemon was not cut, and place in the container. As you fill each lemon with salt, pack it into the container tightly against the other lemons.

When all the lemons have been filled with salt and tightly tucked in the container, pour any remaining salt—including the salt left on the parchment paper—into the container. Ideally, you want to fill the container to the brim with lemons.

If there's much space at the top of the container when you've pushed in every lemon, place a small plate on top of the lemons to hold them down (if your container allows it). For a narrow container, hold down with a large wooden spoon or the bottom of a tall glass. Pour the lemon juice into the container, followed by enough water to cover every lemon completely. Add the bay leaves and peppercorns and put on the lid.

Let the lemons sit in a cool pantry or in an area out of the direct sunlight until tender, for at least 2 weeks. If the lid is tight enough, flip the container every day so that it rests on its lid every other day. Once the lemons are preserved, refrigerate after opening.

MAKES 10 PRESERVED LEMONS

If you puree basil leaves in oil in your blender, then heat and strain the oil, what's left is a pure, fresh-tasting flavored oil that's just right for a salad of heirloom tomatoes (page 112) or for drizzling on soups. Michael Chiarello, the master of infused oil, showed me this great method of intensifying an herb's flavor.

This recipe is simple, but the basil leaves have to be perfectly fresh, and you'll want to use a very good extra-virgin olive oil.

Basil Oil

Put the basil leaves in a blender with the olive oil and process to a smooth puree.

3 cups firmly packed basil leaves

1 1/2 cups extra-virgin olive oil

Pour the basil-oil mixture into a saucepan over medium heat. Once the mixture simmers, let it cook for no more than 45 seconds, or just enough to release the oils in the basil. Pour into a chinois or fine-mesh sieve over a clean bowl. Give the oil time to drain; don't try and push it through the sieve.

If you'd like, strain the oil again through a paper coffee filter. Store the basil oil in an airtight jar, away from direct sunlight.

MAKES 1 1/2 CUPS OIL

RESOURCES

My favorite resource is the farmers' market. If you find just-picked, locally grown vegetables and fruit, your cooking can't help but shine. I've included several contacts for finding specific organic fruits, nuts, and vegetables in your area, as well as shops where I find unusual vinegars, seasonings, and cook's tools. Most of these sources can provide overnight shipping of perishables. Please note that organic, local produce is available only during the growing season. Check with the sources listed below for availability.

Organic Fruits, Vegetables, Nuts, and Grains

California Certified Organic Farmers (CCOF)

www.ccof.org
The CCOF online directory can point you to unusual or hard-to-find varieties of organic vegetables and fruits in your area.

National Farmers' Market Directory

This link gives you a map of the United States; click your state to find the nearest farmers' market.
www.ams.usda.gov/farmersmarkets/map.htm

Veritable Vegetable

This vegetable wholesaler can help you locate hard-to-find organic items, such as red pearl onions.
www.veritablevegetable.com/services.htm

Whole Foods Market

www.wholefoodsmarket.com/products

◆ APRICOTS, NECTARINES, PLUMS, AND PLUOTS ◆

Frog Hollow Farm

P.O. Box 872
Brentwood, CA 94513
(888) 779-4511
www.froghollow.com
Al and Becky Courchesne

◆ FAVA BEANS ◆

Phipp's Country

2700 Pescadero Road
P.O. Box 349
Pescadero, CA 94060
(650) 879-0787
www.phippscountry.com

◆ PISTACHIOS AND WALNUTS ◆

Oliver Family Orchards

www.experienceanut.com
George and Sally Oliver

◆ BLACK RICE AND WILD RICE ◆

The Pasta Shop

5655 College Avenue
Oakland, CA 94618
(888) 952-4005
www.rockridgemarkethall.com

Whole Foods Market

www.wholefoodsmarket.com/products

Cheeses

◆ GREEK CHEESES: FETA, KASSERI, MYZITHRA, MANOURI, AND OTHERS ◆

The Pasta Shop

5655 College Avenue
Oakland, CA 94618
(888) 952-4005
www.rockridgemarkethall.com

◆ FRESH MOZZARELLA ◆

The Mozzarella Company

2944 Elm Street
Dallas, TX 75226
(800) 798-2954
www.mozzco.com
Paula Lambert

Todaro Brothers

555 Second Avenue
New York, NY 10016
(877) 472-2767
www.todarobros.com

NapaStyle

801 Main Street
St. Helena, CA 94574
(866) 776-6272
www.napastyle.com
NapaStyle sells a make-your-own mozzarella kit.

Chocolate

Scharffen Berger Chocolate
914 Heinz Avenue
Berkeley, CA 94710
www.scharffen-berger.com

Duck and Chicken

D'Artagnan
280 Wilson Avenue
Newark, NJ 07105
(800) 327-8246
www.dartagnan.com

Grimaud Farms
1320 South Aurora Street
Stockton, CA 95206
(800) 466-9955
www.grimaud.com

Grape Leaves

The Pasta Shop
5655 College Avenue
Oakland, CA 94618
(888) 952-4005
www.rockridgemarkethall.com

Salami and Sausages

The Pasta Shop
5655 College Avenue
Oakland, CA 94618
(888) 952-4005
www.rockridgemarkethall.com

Seafood

Rockridge Fish
5655 College Avenue
Oakland, CA 94618
(510) 654-3474 (direct line)
(888) 952-4005
www.rockridgemarkethall.com
Carp roe

◆ CLAMS AND MUSSELS ◆

Hog Island Oyster Co.
P.O. Box 829
Marshall, CA 94940
(415) 663-9218
www.hogislandoyster.com

Vinegars, Oils, Salt, and Seasonings

Formaggio Kitchen
244 Huron Avenue
Cambridge, MA 02138
(888) 212-3224
www.formaggiokitchen.com
Banyuls de vinaigre, orange flower water,
vinocotto, wild fennel pollen

NapaStyle
801 Main Street
St. Helena, CA 94574
(866) 776-6272
www.napastyle.com
Gray sea salt and sea salt grinder, fine olive
oils, basil-infused oil, Calabrian chilies in oil

The Pasta Shop
5655 College Avenue
Oakland, CA 94618
(510) 654-3474 (direct line)
(888) 952-4005
www.rockridgemarkethall.com
Sea salt, fine olive oils and vinegars

Cooks' Tools

Dean & Deluca
(877) 826-9246
www.deananddeluca.com

NapaStyle
801 Main Street
St. Helena, CA 94574
(866) 776-6272
www.napastyle.com

Williams-Sonoma
(877) 812-6235
www.williams-sonoma.com

ACKNOWLEDGMENTS

Cat

This book would never have been written without the support of my family. To my mother, Virginia: You taught me to celebrate life and continue to be my inspiration and light. To my father, Spiro: You are my hero. You gave me the roots that hold me up and the family stories that I cherish. To my much better half, Jen: You are my rock; thank you for your constant love and support. I love you always. To my son Zoran, the sun rises and sets on you. To my godparents, Taki and Maria, for showing me that a true lady is gracious, warm, and caring. To my brothers, Mike and Chris, who taught me courage and cunning and gave me the strength to take on the world. To Carrie and Jennifer, thank you for making my brothers happy and bringing Nicholas, Alexandria, Anna, and Andrew into the world and our family; I love and adore you all. To Morgan Cora, who made me an aunt for the first time: Always reach for the stars and know that I am always here for you. To Carla, Randy, and Jeff, for your blessings and love. To Joanne, Jesse, and the family, my Southern connection, for showing such grace. To my aunt Demetra, my uncle Yiorgios, and cousins Yanni and Elleni in Skopelos, Greece, for treasuring my family as we do you. Finally, to all my friends in Jackson, Mississippi, especially, all the Wests, Jim Johnson, and Hank Holmes. Going home is like a cool glass of water. You help me always remember where it is I come from.

I owe many, many thanks to the people who helped create this book. Susie Heller, my surrogate godmother. My agent, Doe Coover, who first believed in me and my book, and persuaded others to believe in me as well. Bill LeBlond, for whom I have the greatest respect and admiration; thank you, Bill, for taking a chance on me. Ann Krueger Spivack, a brilliant writer who's become a dear friend; thank you for giving this book its direction. Terry Paetzold, my first pastry chef, who tested and tasted my recipes with unflagging enthusiasm; it's been my good luck to have you as a friend since we first began working together. (And thanks to Terry's family, especially Ray, who got to taste everything two or three times!) Thanks to Amy Burlaga Vogler for all of her help in the early mornings.

Maren Caruso was incredible to work with. She brings out the light of everyone in a room. Thanks also to Faiza Ali, Kim Konecny, Erin Quon, and Hilary Brodey for a perfect photo shoot.

Everyone at Chronicle Books was a pleasure to work with. Thank you Vivien Sung, Amy Treadwell, Holly Burrows, Jan Hughes, Doug Ogan, and Steve Kim.

Thanks to David Dodson, my guru, invaluable advisor, and friend, for your unconditional guidance and truth.

Since culinary school, my bond with Lori Lynn Bauer ("Where are all the coffee cups?") has sustained me many times. Lori, you are a friend in the truest sense of the word.

Thanks to my friend and advocate, Tida Beattie, who brings her energy and balance to every project. Your tireless quest for knowledge and challenge inspires me.

Beverly Hanapole has watched me grow, helping me with an open heart from my very first days in New York.

Catrina Lembo Di Martini and Randy Di Martini have always been there for me—their support and love have never wavered.

Lucy Bowen and Bruce Taylor are my friends through thick and thin. Months can go by and when we connect, we pick up right where we left off.

I am grateful to Sara Corpening Whiteford and Mary Corpening Barber for the many times they've offered help. You inspire me to pay it forward as often as possible.

Thanks to Kelly and David Magna for the big, beautiful smiles you always have for me.

To Bonnie Light and Bettie Cally, a big thank-you for all the dinners and the shoulder to cry on. Only with true friends can I do that.

Thank you to Donna and Giovanni Scala who welcomed me to the Napa Valley with open arms, gave me my first job in California, and taught me the art of caramelization.

Michael Chiarello taught me many lessons—on cooking, and on opening a restaurant, but especially about life and how to live it. I relished my time spent at Tra Vigne and opening Postino with you.

The many passionate people at Tra Vigne have been so good to me over the years. Many thanks to Kevin Cronin, Michael Gyetvan, Tony Prince, Carmen Quagliata, Joey Scarpone, and Michael Laukert.

Thanks to Mariano Orlando, my Sicilian friend. You are a special person in my life and I have the utmost love and respect for you.

With much gratitude to Georges Blanc, one of the two chefs who allowed me to apprentice with him in Vonnas in the Le Bresse region of France. Working with this master of cuisine changed how I look at food.

Roger Verge had a hug for me every day when I apprenticed at Moulin de Mougins. He, his wife, Denise, and his chef, Serge, left an imprint on my life through their farms, their food, and wine. His love of the good life has stayed with me.

Thanks to my great Napa friend Monique Nelson from Joseph Phelps.

Thanks to Scott France, who shares my passion for both food and film. Filming our documentary was a highlight of my career.

Laura Buckley, trusted partner and director and one of the most creative women I know. If I had to choose one person to work beside me on a grueling, exciting project, I'd pick you.

Charles Rudnick, you are as genuine as the day is long and that, to me, is priceless. Thank you for helping me realize a dream.

Joan Zoloth, whenever I need for someone "to make it happen," you're the one.

Larry Bain, whose boundless energy to make the world better is contagious. You introduced me to sustainability and I will be forever thankful.

Thanks to the brilliant *Cat Cora Show* team—Joanne Greene, Adam Lerner, Jessica Chatham, Darby Smith, Ricardo Kovacs, Dan Hayes, and Stefan Welter—you helped make my dream a reality.

A heartfelt thanks to all the chefs, restaurateurs, and vintners who have given me help, advice, and much more over the years: Elizabeth Faulkner, Jan Birnbaum, Thomas Keller, Traci Des Jardin, Tori Ritchie, Joey Altman, Jennifer Cox, Tanya Holland, Hollis Grant, David Gingrass, Brannin Beal, Emily Luchetti, Pat Kuleto, Kelsie, Cal, Chris, Alice, and the inspiring crew at Chez Panisse.

Thank you to the staff and my customers at Postino, who made me feel good every day about my own vision and who made my years at Postino fly by.

Thank you to Jacques Pépin for sending a letter on my behalf to the James Beard House after tasting a meal that I cooked at Bistro Don Giovanni. Jacques has been a constant source of inspiration since I began cooking.

Thank you, Marion Cunnigham. You guided me when I was still wet behind the ears. Your shining example has always been a source of inner strength for me.

Much gratitude to Julia Child, who kindly took the time to talk to me many years ago. Her advice to attend the Culinary Institute of America was the first step of my career. To me, you are a First Lady, and your love of food has inspired and paved the way for so many other cooks.

To Larry Forgione, I owe a great debt for an incredible first work experience, cooking in an exciting New York restaurant. You've treated me with complete respect and I will always be grateful.

Thanks to Melissa Kelly, one of the most passionate chefs I know. Much of the foundation for my skills was built during my time working with you. You rock.

Thanks to Cindy Pawlcyn for the many times you served as my mentor and my friend; when I needed you, you were always there.

Thanks to Wendy Levy, who is talented on so many levels—making food, making films, and as restaurateur and friend.

For teaching me how to bet on a horse, thanks to Kerri Heffernan, talented chef, restaurateur, and friend.

To all my friends at Food Network, whose support was constant: Judy Girard, Eileen Opatut, Bob Tuschman, Alison Page, Irene Wong, Suzanne Schecter, Kate Rados, Adam Rockwell, Susan Stockton, and all the great culinary and production crews I had the good fortune to work with.

This book wouldn't be complete without a thank-you to Barbara Tropp. When I was a young, scared chef at Bistro Don Giovanni, Barbara called me over every time she and her husband came into the restaurant. "You're doing great," she'd say, patting me on the arm, and her words of encouragement have stayed with me all these years. Barbara, you are much loved and truly missed.

Thanks to Jaime Wolf, for watching my back. You're the best.

To Belle and Barney Rhodes, who served as my Napa Valley grandparents when I first arrived in California. I will always treasure our time spent together.

This book would not have been written without all the help Robin Mills has given me over the years.

My first experiences with the big-time culinary world were with Kim Yorio and Caitlin Connelly, who guided me with such grace and caring.

Thank you to Jim Lebeouf, Tom and Barbara Wolf, and the J & L Enterprise Staff for believing in my visions.

Thanks to Nancy Banks for your great sense of humor while working on my psyche. All your efforts are finally paying off.

Thanks to Bob Burke for all the coffee meetings and for helping me to understand the finances and everyday operations of running a successful restaurant.

Heidi Gintner makes the space around me beautiful with her kind spirit as well as her exceptional sense of style.

Lorraine Battle adds finesse to everything she touches, and shares a great wit, which I love.

Thanks to Nick Boer for giving me the opportunity to write my "Cooking from the Hip" column for the Contra Costa Times. You and your crew are a blast to work with and you have been a good friend.

Thanks to Tietjen Fischer, my styling Buddha, for making me wanna be better styled.

Thanks to the guys at Taxi Films, I love ya.

My branding team, Bonnie Wan-Rees and Mari Cortizo-Burgess, helped hone my vision, giving it both direction and clarity.

Thanks to the Owen family and the "neighborhood" for keeping it real with me.

Thanks to Rocco DiSpirito, my co-host on my first Food Network show. The fact that I was silly and you were serious meant great chemistry for our show and our friendship. Thanks for showing me the ropes and being a friend to this day.

It was scary as hell for a Mississippi gal to live and work in Manhattan for the first time. Anne Rosenzweig made it a lot less scary and I will always be indebted to her for that. Anne, I'm grateful for your belief in me and the wonderful experiences I had working with you.

Thanks to SC Johnson for hiring me to endorse their product and treating me like royalty; to McCormick, for your continued belief in my ability to represent your product; to Claire Burke and Hunter Public Relations, for always being my advocate.

• • • •

Ann

While writing about the Cora family, I was welcomed with open arms by Cat, Jennifer, Virginia, and Spiro, whose warmth and graciousness made working on this book a pleasure. Cat, thank you for the smoothies, the tea, Alma's mustard, and most of all for sharing your family stories with me. Thanks to Susie Heller, for giving me heart, always.

Many thanks to the kind people at Chronicle Books: Bill LeBlond, Amy Treadwell, Holly Burrows, Jan Hughes, Vivien Sung, Doug Ogan, and Steve Kim. Thanks to Carrie Bradley for her thoughtful, thorough, and considerate copyedit. Thanks to Doe Coover and Frances Kennedy. Thanks to Maren Caruso, Faiza Ali, Kim Konecny, Erin Quon, and Hilary Brodey.

My down-the-street family, Suzie, Steven, Becca, and Rae Sullivan sustained me with Rae & Rachey sleepovers, Christmas tea, and New Year's Eve dinners. Showing their usual impeccable timing, they whisked my kids off camping as soon as the proofs for this book arrived. My across-the-street family, Denise, Aleco, Dimitri, and Argyro "Loula" Georges welcomed my entire family as only Greeks can to their Easter celebration. *Argyro* means gold in Greek, and Loula truly fits her name. Thank you, Georges, for not laughing (too much) at my pronunciation of *galatoboureko*.

My dear friend Maria "Tia Connie" Bautista energetically kid-herded at more than one farmers' market. Jennifer Bowman Nauts French is always at the ready with coffee, sympathy, just-picked cucumbers, and wine grape jelly. Pam Utz, Don Roberts, Gary Jones, Elaine Anderson, Elspeth Martin, and Chuck Williams have inspired me in countless ways since Pam hired me for my first job at Williams-Sonoma fifteen years ago. Michael Chiarello made me a part of his NapaStyle family, and showed his generosity each time I got the chance to work with him.

Thanks to my parents, Pat and Elton Krueger, for their love and support; to my grandmother Virginia Roberts Krueger, for sharing her love of good food; and to my grandmother Gertrude Clark Fleming, for sharing her love of reading. Thanks to my aunts Carolyn Roffino and Beba Krueger de Chapa for their great warmth and sense of style. Thanks to all the Kruegers and all the Spivacks: Burt and Sandy, Sue and Steve, Wendy and Charlie, Mary and Fred, Poppy and Tim, Sheila and Mike. Thanks especially to my favorite sous chef, Rachel Spivack, for her kitchen dance breaks; to Danny Spivack, my favorite Greek festival and *loukamathes*-tasting buddy; and Brad Spivack, for his constant loyalty and his great laugh.

• • • •

Index

A

Achibades, 121

Aegean Meatballs with Pita Bread, 78

Agginares skaras kappori saltsa, 173

Aioli

Caper Aioli, 173

Tangerine Aioli, 94

Alma's Fruited Mustard, 176

Alma's Sweet-Hot Mustard, 187

Almonds

Greek Butter Cookies, 48–49

Honey-Dipped Cookies with
Fresh Figs, 72–73

Olive Oil Cake, 22

Orange-Scented Almond Cookies, 96

Rolled Baklava, 81

toasting, 30

Amygthalota me portakali, 96

Anginares me latholemono, 57

Arni kai myzithra Skopelos, 156–57

Arni tis skaras me moustartha, 176

Artichokes

Artichoke Hearts Braised in
Lemon Juice, 57

Grilled Artichokes with Caper
Aioli, 173

Arugula, Salt-Roasted Beets,
and Endive Salad, 145

Asparagus, Grilled, with
Tangerine Aioli, 94

Avocados

Avocado Salsa, 133

Crab and Avocado "Sandwiches"
with Mango Coulis, 133

B

Baked Eggplant with Meat and
Béchamel Sauce, 167–68

Baked Stuffed Onions, 125

Baklava, Rolled, 81

Baklava orthi, 81

Banana-Coconut Cream Pie, 116–17

Banyuls vinegar, 112

Basil Oil, 189

Beans

Pampered White Beans, 92

Stewed Green Beans with
Fresh Oregano, 37

Béchamel Sauce, 167–68

Beef

Aegean Meatballs with Pita Bread, 78

Baked Eggplant with Meat and
Béchamel Sauce, 167–68

Bell Peppers Stuffed with Meat
and Rice, 46

brisket, smoking tips for, 44

Spiro's Brisket, 43

Beets, Salt-Roasted, Arugula,
and Endive Salad, 145

Bell peppers

Bell Peppers Stuffed with Meat
and Rice, 46

roasting, 135

Salsa Rosa, 134–35

Blanc, Georges, 85

Bougatsa, 161, 169

Bread

Aegean Meatballs with Pita Bread, 78

Fish Roe Spread with Crostini, 34–35

Lamb-and-Cheese-Stuffed Sandwiches,
156–57

Pork Skewers with Pita Bread, 42

Rustic Kalamata Olive Bread, 102

Skillet Leek Pizza, 165–66

Taki's Cured Sardines with Tomatoes, Olives, and Bread, 162–63

Tomato Bread Soup, 90

Breaded Veal with Tomatoes, Garlic, and Basil Brown Butter, 122

Broccoli Rabe, Spicy, 137

Brothers, Alma, 13, 176, 187

Brussels Sprouts, Caramelized, 19

Butter and Cheese Noodles, 18

C

Cabbage Leaves Filled with Lamb and Rice, 79

Cake, Olive Oil, 22

Capers, 77

Caper Aioli, 173

Caramelized Brussels Sprouts, 19

Shrimp and Caper Salad, 77

Caramelized Brussels Sprouts, 19

Cheese

Baked Stuffed Onions, 125

Banana-Coconut Cream Pie, 116–17

Butter and Cheese Noodles, 18

Fava Bean–Mint Ravioli with Fava Bean–Mint Pesto, 123–24

Grilled Grape Leaves Filled with Goat Cheese, 104–5

Grilled Stonefruit with Prosciutto and Sheep's Cheese, 181

Lamb-and-Cheese-Stuffed Sandwiches, 156–57

Polenta with Fontina and Parmesan, 70

shavings, 145, 181

Skillet Leek Pizza, 165–66

Spicy Feta Spread, 59

Spinach, Dill, and Feta Baked in Phyllo Dough, 55–56

Strawberry-Topped Vanilla Custards, 107–8

Summer's First Heirloom Tomatoes with Fresh Mozzarella, 112

Tomato, Cucumber, and Feta Salad, 21

Watermelon, Feta, and Mint Salad, 158

Cherries

Alma's Fruited Mustard, 176

Sour Cherry Torte, 61–62

Chiarello, Michael, 119, 189

Chicken

Chicken Stewed in Wine, Garlic, and Cinnamon, 16

Classic Greek Roasted Chicken with Lemon and Herbs, 35

Harvest Chicken with Vinocotto, 106

Roasted Chicken Stock, 184

Chiffonade, 112

Child, Julia, 11

Chilies

arbol, 186

Calabrian, 134

roasting, 135

Chocolate Ganache, Warm, over Coffee Ice Cream, 127–28

Church-Style Lemon-Roasted Potatoes, 36

Clams, Manila, with Fennel-Cured Salami, 121

Classic Greek Roasted Chicken with Lemon and Herbs, 35

Coffee Ice Cream, Terry's, 128

Cookies

Greek Butter Cookies, 48–49

Honey-Dipped Cookies with Fresh Figs, 72–73

Orange-Scented Almond Cookies, 96

Corn Zabaglione, Sweet, 115

Costas, Peter J. "Taki," 131, 161

Crab

Crab and Avocado "Sandwiches" with Mango Coulis, 133

Split Lobster Stuffed with Crabmeat, 136

Cremosas, 107–8

Croquettes, Tomato, with Cucumber Yogurt, 155

Crostini, Fish Roe Spread with, 34–35

Cucumbers

Cucumber Yogurt, 58

Tomato, Cucumber, and Feta Salad, 21

Cunningham, Marion, 11

Custard

Custard-Filled Phyllo Triangles, 169

Strawberry-Topped Vanilla Custards, 107–8

D

Dolmathes me arni kai rizi, 79

Dolmathestis skara me tiri, 104–5

Domates yemistes, 80

Domatokeftethes me tzatziki, 155

Domato soupa me psomi, 90

Duck Breasts, Muscovy, with Black Rice, Pistachios, and Orange, 146

E

Eggplant, Baked, with Meat and Béchamel Sauce, 167–68

Eliopita, 102

Endive, Salt-Roasted Beets, and Arugula Salad, 145

F

Fassolia, 92

Fassoulakia yahni, 37

Fava beans

buying, 123

Fava Bean–Mint Ravioli with Fava Bean–Mint Pesto, 123–24

shelling, 123

Fennel

pollen, wild, 101

Spring Onion, Fennel, and Potato Soup, 26

Whole Fish Roasted with Fennel, Olives, and Chilies, 87

Figs, Honey-Dipped Cookies with Fresh, 72–73

Fish

buying fresh, 89

Fish Roe Spread with Crostini, 34–35

Pan-Seared Halibut with Sweet Corn Zabaglione, 113

Taki's Cured Sardines with Tomatoes, Olives, and Bread, 162–63

Whole Fish Roasted with Fennel, Olives, and Chilies, 87

Forgione, Larry, 85

Fresh Fruit Tart, 139–40

Fresh Spinach with Preserved Lemons, 71

Fruits. *See also individual fruits*

Fresh Fruit Tart, 139–40

Grilled Stonefruit with Prosciutto and Sheep's Cheese, 181

G

Galatoboureko, 13, 38–39

Ganache, Chocolate, 128

Garides tis skaras avgolemono, 174

Garithosalata me kappari, 77

Gelato, Vanilla, 148

Grape leaves

Grilled Grape Leaves Filled with Goat Cheese, 104–5

rolling, 105

Grapes

Harvest Chicken with Vinocotto, 106

Greek Butter Cookies, 48–49

Greek Potato Salad, 45

Greens, Southern-Style, 28

Grilled Artichokes with Caper Aioli, 173

Grilled Asparagus with Tangerine Aioli, 94

Grilled Grape Leaves Filled with Goat Cheese, 104–5

Grilled Lamb Chops with Alma's Fruited Mustard, 176

Grilled Prawns with Egg and Lemon Froth, 174

Grilled Stonefruit with Prosciutto and Sheep's Cheese, 181

Gyetvan, Michael, 119

H

Halibut, Pan-Seared, with Sweet Corn Zabaglione, 113

Harvest Chicken with Vinocotto, 106

Hirino psito, 27

Honey-Dipped Cookies with Fresh Figs, 72–73

Horiatiki, 15, 21

Horta, 28

Htipiti, 59

I

Ice baths, 139

Ice cream

Prunes and Armagnac with Vanilla Gelato, 148

Terry's Coffee Ice Cream, 128

Warm Chocolate Ganache over Coffee Ice Cream, 127–28

K

Karithi tarta, 30–31

Keftethakia kai pita, 78

Kelly, Melissa, 85

Kota kapama, 13, 15, 16

Koto me vinocotto, 106

Kotopoulo psito, 35

Kouneli stifatho, 67–68

Kourambiedes, 41, 48–49

Kremithes yemista, 125

L

Lamb

Bell Peppers Stuffed with Meat and Rice, 46

Cabbage Leaves Filled with Lamb and Rice, 79

Grilled Lamb Chops with Alma's Fruited Mustard, 176

Lamb-and-Cheese-Stuffed Sandwiches, 156–57

Lathi torte, 22

Leek Pizza, Skillet, 165–66

Lemons

Artichoke Hearts Braised in Lemon Juice, 57

Church-Style Lemon-Roasted Potatoes, 36

Classic Greek Roasted Chicken with Lemon and Herbs, 35

Grilled Prawns with Egg and Lemon Froth, 174

Preserved Lemons, 188

zesting, 22

Lobster, Split, Stuffed with Crabmeat, 136

M

Makaronia, 18

Mangos

cutting, 133

Mango Coulis, 133

Manila Clams with Fennel-Cured Salami, 121

Manitaria tursi, 186

Meat Sauce, 167–68

Melomakarona kai sika, 72–73

Milk Pie, 38–39

Mondavi, Robert, 85

Moussaka, 167–68

Muscovy Duck Breasts with Black Rice, Pistachios, and Orange, 146

Mushrooms, Pickled, 186

Mussels, Spicy Gypsy, 101

Mustard

Alma's Fruited Mustard, 176

Alma's Sweet-Hot Mustard, 187

Mythias, 101

O

Oil, Basil, 189

Olives

Olive Oil Cake, 22

Rustic Kalamata Olive Bread, 102

Taki's Cured Sardines with Tomatoes, Olives, and Bread, 162–63

Whole Fish Roasted with Fennel, Olives, and Chilies, 87

Onions

Baked Stuffed Onions, 125

Spring Onion, Fennel, and Potato Soup, 26

Stewed Rabbit with Pearl Onions, 67–68

Oranges

Muscovy Duck Breast with Black Rice, Pistachios, and Orange, 146

Orange-Scented Almond Cookies, 96

zesting, 22

Orlando, Mariano, 119

Ouzo, 101

P

Paetzold, Terry, 127

Pampered White Beans, 92

Panko crumbs, 122

Pan-Seared Halibut with Sweet Corn Zabaglione, 113

Pantzaria salata, 145

Pasta

Butter and Cheese Noodles, 18

Fava Bean–Mint Ravioli with Fava Bean–Mint Pesto, 123–24

Pastry Cream, 139–40

Patates lemonates, 36

Patates me lemone, 178

Patatosalata, 41, 45

Patatosoupa, 26

Pecans

Custard-Filled Phyllo Triangles, 169

Honey-Dipped Cookies with Fresh Figs, 72–73

toasting, 30

Pépin, Jacques, 11, 85

Pesto, Fava Bean–Mint, 124

Phyllo dough

Custard-Filled Phyllo Triangles, 169

Milk Pie, 38–39

Rolled Baklava, 81

Spinach, Dill, and Feta Baked in Phyllo Dough, 55–56

tips for, 39

Pickled Mushrooms, 186

Pies

Banana-Coconut Cream Pie, 116–17

Milk Pie, 38–39

Pine nuts, toasting, 80

Piperies yemistes me kima kai rizi, 46

Polenta with Fontina and Parmesan, 70

Pork

Pork Skewers with Pita Bread, 42

Slow-Roasted Pork with Bourbon, 27

Potatoes

Church-Style Lemon-Roasted Potatoes, 36

Greek Potato Salad, 45

Skopelos-Style Grilled Potatoes, 178

Spring Onion, Fennel, and Potato Soup, 26

Prawns. *See* **Shrimp and prawns**

Preserved Lemons, 188

Prosciutto, Grilled Stonefruit with Sheep's Cheese and, 181

Prunes and Armagnac with Vanilla Gelato, 148

Psari psito, 87

Q

Quagliata, Carmen, 119

R

Rabbit, Stewed, with Pearl Onions, 67–68

Ravioli, Fava Bean–Mint, with Fava Bean–Mint Pesto, 123–24

Rice

Bell Peppers Stuffed with Meat and Rice, 46

black, 146

Cabbage Leaves Filled with Lamb and Rice, 79

Muscovy Duck Breasts with Black Rice, Pistachios, and Orange, 146

Skopeletti Stuffed Tomatoes, 80

Spinach, Dill, and Feta Baked in Phyllo Dough, 55–56

Roasted Chicken Stock, 184

Roasted Veal Stock, 185

Rolled Baklava, 81

Rustic Kalamata Olive Bread, 102

S

Salads

Greek Potato Salad, 45

Salt-Roasted Beets, Arugula, and Endive Salad, 145

Shrimp and Caper Salad, 77

Summer's First Heirloom Tomatoes with Fresh Mozzarella, 112

Tomato, Cucumber, and Feta Salad, 21

Watermelon, Feta, and Mint Salad, 158

Salami, Fennel-Cured, Manila Clams with, 121

Salsas

Avocado Salsa, 133

Salsa Rosa, 134–35

Salt-Roasted Beets, Arugula, and Endive Salad, 145

Sandwiches, Lamb-and-Cheese-Stuffed, 156–57

Sardeles takis, 162–63

Sardines, Taki's Cured, with Tomatoes, Olives, and Bread, 162–63

Sauces

Béchamel Sauce, 167–68

Caper Aioli, 173

Chocolate Ganache, 128

Fava Bean–Mint Pesto, 124

Mango Coulis, 133

Meat Sauce, 167–68

Tangerine Aioli, 94

Scarpone, Joey, 119

Shrimp and prawns

Grilled Prawns with Egg and Lemon Froth, 174

Prawns in Grappa Cream Sauce with Salsa Rosa, 134–35

Shrimp and Caper Salad, 77

Skewers, Pork, with Pita Bread, 42

Skillet Leek Pizza, 165–66

Skopeletti Stuffed Tomatoes, 80

Skopelos-Style Grilled Potatoes, 178

Slow-Roasted Pork with Bourbon, 27

Soups

Spring Onion, Fennel, and Potato Soup, 26

Tomato Bread Soup, 90

Sour Cherry Torte, 61–62

Southern-Style Greens, 28

Souvlaki me pita, 42

Spanaki me lemone, 71

Spanakopita, 55–56

Sparangi tis skaras me mantarini saltsa, 94

Spicy Broccoli Rabe, 137

Spicy Feta Spread, 59

Spicy Gypsy Mussels, 101

Spinach

Fresh Spinach with Preserved Lemons, 71

Spinach, Dill, and Feta Baked in Phyllo Dough, 55–56

Spiro's Brisket, 43

Split Lobster Stuffed with Crabmeat, 136

Spreads

Fish Roe Spread with Crostini, 34–35

Spicy Feta Spread, 59

Spring Onion, Fennel, and Potato Soup, 26

Stewed Green Beans with Fresh Oregano, 37

Stewed Rabbit with Pearl Onions, 67–68

Stifatho, 65, 67–68

Stocks

Roasted Chicken Stock, 184

Roasted Veal Stock, 185

Strawberry-Topped Vanilla Custards, 107–8

Summer's First Heirloom Tomatoes with Fresh Mozzarella, 112

Sweet Corn Zabaglione, 115

T

Taki's Cured Sardines with Tomatoes, Olives, and Bread, 162–63

Tangerine Aioli, 94

Taramosalata, 34–35

Tarts

Fresh Fruit Tart, 139–40

Walnut Tart, 30–31

Tempering, 79

Terry's Coffee Ice Cream, 128

Tiganopita me praso, 165–66

Tomatoes

Bell Peppers Stuffed with Meat and Rice, 46

Breaded Veal with Tomatoes, Garlic, and Basil Brown Butter, 122

heirloom, 111

Salsa Rosa, 134–35

Skopeletti Stuffed Tomatoes, 80

Spicy Gypsy Mussels, 101

Stewed Green Beans with Fresh Oregano, 37

Summer's First Heirloom Tomatoes with Fresh Mozzarella, 112

Taki's Cured Sardines with Tomatoes, Olives, and Bread, 162–63

Tomato Bread Soup, 90

Tomato Croquettes with Cucumber Yogurt, 155

Tomato, Cucumber, and Feta Salad, 21

Torte, Sour Cherry, 61–62

Tortes me vissino glyko, 61–62

Tzatziki, 58

V

Vanila pagato me thamaskino ke Armagnac, 155

Vanilla Gelato, 148

Veal

Breaded Veal with Tomatoes, Garlic, and Basil Brown Butter, 122

Roasted Veal Stock, 185

Vergé, Roger, 85

Vinocotto, Harvest Chicken with, 106

Vitello scallopini, 122

Vodino spiros, 43

W

Walnuts

Custard-Filled Phyllo Triangles, 169

Rolled Baklava, 81

toasting, 30

Walnut Tart, 30–31

Warm Chocolate Ganache over Coffee Ice Cream, 127–28

Watermelon, Feta, and Mint Salad, 158

Whole Fish Roasted with Fennel, Olives, and Chilies, 87

Y

Yogurt, Cucumber, 58

Z

Zabaglione, Sweet Corn, 115

Zesting, 22

Zouboukos, Pete and Jimmy, 33, 36

TABLE OF EQUIVALENTS

The exact equivalents in the following tables have been rounded for convenience.

LIQUID/DRY MEASURES

U.S.	Metric
$1/4$ teaspoon	1.25 milliliters
$1/2$ teaspoon	2.5 milliliters
1 teaspoon	5 milliliters
1 tablespoon (3 teaspoons)	15 milliliters
1 fluid ounce (2 tablespoons)	30 milliliters
$1/4$ cup	60 milliliters
$1/3$ cup	80 milliliters
$1/2$ cup	120 milliliters
1 cup	240 milliliters
1 pint (2 cups)	480 milliliters
1 quart (4 cups, 32 ounces)	960 milliliters
1 gallon (4 quarts)	3.84 liters
1 ounce (by weight)	28 grams
1 pound	454 grams
2.2 pounds	1 kilogram

OVEN TEMPERATURE

Fahrenheit	Celsius	Gas
250	120	$1/2$
275	140	1
300	150	2
325	160	3
350	180	4
375	190	5
400	200	6
425	220	7
450	230	8
475	240	9
500	260	10

LENGTH

U.S.	Metric
$1/4$ inch	6 millimeters
$1/2$ inch	12 millimeters
1 inch	2.5 centimeters